BLACK WORKER IN THE DEEP SOUTH

Black Worker in the Deep South

A Personal Record

by HOSEA HUDSON

INTERNATIONAL PUBLISHERS
New York

Dedication

I want to dedicate this book to my little late wife Vaganina Larue, who longed to see this book printed in her lifetime. She would always remind of her friends that I had written a book to be printed and that it would be printed someday.

Library of Congress Cataloging-in-Publication Data

Hudson, Hosea.
  Black worker in the Deep South: a personal record. 1st ed.
New York, International Publishers, 1972. 2nd ed., 1991.

  x, 130 p. 21 cm. $4.95

  1. Hudson, Hosea. 2. Afro-American Communists—Southern States—Biography. 3. Afro-Americans—Southern States—Biography. 4. Afro-Americans—Economic conditions—Southern States. 5. Trade unions—Southern States--Afro-American membership. I. Title

HX84.H8A32   331.6'3'96073075   72–82078
                          [B]   MARC

Library of Congress   72[r79]rev
ISBN 10: 0-7178-0683-9 2nd ed. Pbk   ISBN 13: 978-0-7178-0683-6

CONTENTS

INTRODUCTION   vii
by Scott Douglas

1. PLOWHAND IN THE GEORGIA
   COTTON FIELDS   1

2. SHARECROPPERS ARE ALWAYS
   MOVING   13

3. PLOWHAND INTO INDUSTRIAL
   WORKER   19

4. LEGAL LYNCHINGS   30

5. THE MAKING OF A UNION MAN
   AND A COMMUNIST   36

6. BOSSES AND STOOLPIGEONS   43

7. UNEMPLOYMENT STRUGGLES   54

8. VICTORIES AND SETBACKS   60

9. SOUTHERN WORKERS ORGANIZE   72

10. TARGET OF BOSSES AND THE KLAN   84

11. CAMPAIGN TO REGISTER AND VOTE   92

12. MY EDUCATION CONTINUES   101

13. OBSERVATIONS AND TRIBUTES   111

14. THEN AND NOW   122

"As I see it. . ."

These words often prefaced Hosea Hudson's remarks to any audience, large or small, willing to hear his views concerning developments in the community, or national and international arenas. Grounded in his own courageous struggles against the heavy-handed repression of southern capitalists, of Jim Crow segregation, and his own illiteracy, Hosea's view was not one to be ignored.

From his early years of striving to eke a livelihood for his family from the unyielding clay of Georgia, through his later years of organizing to wrest gains for workers from the equally obstinate owners of Birmingham's foundries, Hosea's life personified the struggle of southern Black workers for dignity and justice. Even more, Hosea's life epitomized the convergence of three dynamic currents that continue to leave their mark on the course of history: the African-American struggle for dignity and justice, the emerging southern section of the trade union movement, and the liberating ideas of socialism.

To fully appreciate Hudson's courage, one must view southern life through the grossly distorted prism of Jim Crow segregation. As under today's repressive governments in Central America, the South, too, had its "disappearances"—Black people who had run afoul of the irrationalities of segregation vanished, never to be seen again. Some fled "up North" or to other communities in the South; others were lynched. Not unlike apartheid South Africa, when justice wasn't absolutely elusive for African American southerners, it was absolutely arbitrary. Against the same great odds that paralyzed many who remained less convinced of the prospects for change, Hosea Hudson's story reveals an inventive and visionary sharecropper/foundryman, one able to build movements, enlist allies, and empower men and women, Black and white, in the pursuit of equality and liberation.

On the morning of Tuesday, February 28, 1980, the city council chambers of Birmingham, Alabama were overflowing. Birmingham's then newly elected first African-American mayor, Richard Arrington, Jr., had just awarded the key to the City to Hosea Hudson, and the standing room only, mostly African-American audience had risen to its feet in thunderous, prolonged applause in response to Hosea's acceptance speech.

This enthusiasm had been triggered by Hosea's chapter and verse recital of the foundations of the movement that had led Birmingham out of the shackles of its bestially racist past. Hosea's talk had not been about the heroic civil rights struggles of the 1960s, nor about the 1970s movement against police brutality that produced Birmingham's first Black mayor. Instead, Hosea—sharecropper, foundryman, union organizer, quartet singer, communist—introduced most of the audience, for the first time, to the struggles of the 1930s and 1940s that helped forge the unity and resolve of Birmingham's working class, African-American communities.

Hosea had shared with them their own untold history of struggles, victories and setbacks. They had risen for themselves, as much as for Hosea, in celebration of the roots of Birmingham's progress.

Hounded unmercifully by the FBI, targeted for certain violence by Birmingham's infamous Eugene "Bull" Connor, and persecuted by his employers, Hosea Hudson's pilgrimage for justice remains a lesson in working-class vigilance for today's generation. With class allegiance as his "North Star," and his love for his people to light his path, the repressive forces of his day proved unable to silence his booming voice or contain, much less still, his fighting spirit.

Echoing from churches to union halls, from foundries to the streets, Hosea's voice is remembered in Birmingham as one that railed against the prevailing injustices, one that beckoned a class and a people to unite for their own good.

Black Worker in the Deep South, however, is more than a story of how Hosea Hudson saw the world. It remains a testament to what he did, over a lifetime of struggle, to change it.

Scott Douglas

President, 6th CD Chapter
Alabama New South Coalition
Birmingham, 1991

City of Birmingham
Alabama

PROCLAMATION

WHEREAS,   It is appropriate that an occasion of the significance of "Black
History Month" not pass without tribute to the many unsung heroes
of local history. One such hero is Hosea Hudson; and,

WHEREAS,   Born in Wilkes County, Georgia in 1898, Hosea Hudson moved his family
to Birmingham in 1924 seeking work. Hosea's activities for more than
30 years spanned the breadth of the Afro-American struggle for
democratic rights. Hudson was a builder of the United Steelworkers of
America, holding such posts as recording secretary of Local #1489,
President of Local #2815, and delegate to the Birmingham Industrial
Council; and,

WHEREAS,   Mr. Hudson helped initiate the Right to Vote Club in 1938, which
conducted classes among black people to help them surmount registration
obstacles at the Courthouse. Not limiting his commitment to blacks,
Hudson gave leadership to the Workers' Alliance, which organized poor
whites to register and vote. Hudsons's activities and political beliefs
earned him the enmity of Eugene "Bull" Connor, who was to later gain
national infamy, and was forced to leave Birmingham; and,

WHEREAS,   Today Mr. Hudson lives in Atlantic City, New Jersey and is active in
his community with citizens, young and old, Black and White in the
common struggle for a better life; and,

WHEREAS,   The life of Hosea Hudson has generated two books: "Black Worker in the
South," printed in 1972; and "The Narrative of Hosea Hudson," recently
published by the Harvard University Press; and,

WHEREAS,   Illiterate over half of his life, but not unlearned, Hudson's odyssey
is part and parcel of the heroic, and sometimes bitter, Birmingham
story.

NOW, THEREFORE, I, RICHARD ARRINGTON, JR., Mayor of the City of Birmingham, Alabama do hereby proclaim February 26, 1980, as

HOSEA HUDSON DAY

in the City of Birmingham.

IN WITNESS WHEREOF, I have hereunto set my
hand and caused the Seal of the City of
Birmingham, Alabama to be affixed this the
26ᵗʰ day of February, 1980.

Richard Arrington Jr.
Mayor

BLACK WORKER IN THE DEEP SOUTH

1

PLOWHAND IN THE GEORGIA COTTON FIELDS

My early years were spent on farms in the cotton fields of Wilkes and Oglethorpe Counties in the Black Belt of Georgia. My father and mother were separated when I was a small child and my brother Eddie was a babe in arms. At that time my grandmother, Julia Smith, came to our house with my young Aunt Georgia May to help my mother. And when I was around five, my grandparents' marriage broke up too, partly because grandmother wanted to take us back home with her and my grandfather didn't want to be responsible for the whole family. So the rest of us lived together until Aunt Georgia May married, at the age of nineteen. Georgia May had been my grandmother's plowhand since she was fifteen, and when I was not much more than ten I became her assistant.

My little brother and I, lying on the pinewood floor of a lonesome plantation shack in the dark Georgia nights, used to shiver at the thought of many imaginary dangers, but none of these could be worse than some of the terrifying experiences of our actual life. Like the time when 17 men came to get my Uncle Ned at my grandmother's house, all set to lynch him.

We were living at the time in a two-room log cabin with chimneys at the north and south ends and an open hall in the middle. That night we were all in the north room because a big storm was building up and we felt more sheltered there.

Just before the wind and rain hit the house, a mob of

white men on horses came galloping into the yard. Someone in the crowd hollered, "Let's go round the house!" Minutes later the mob crowded up in the hall outside.

"Put out the lamp," my mother whispered. But my grandmother opened the door and just stood there. She was about five feet tall, weighed 100 pounds and wore a number four shoe.

A tall, husky man, Bob Moon, stood facing her with a shotgun.

"What's you-all looking for?" she asked.

"Ned," they hollered.

She asked what Ned had done, and Bold Bunch, one of the mob, spoke up, "He's been talking about my sister Sallibet."

Uncle Ned cried out, "That's a lie!"

Grandmother made a grab for Bob Moon's shotgun, but he held it high above her head. She told them if they took Ned they'd take him over her dead body. One of them said they didn't want to "hurt" any of the family. "We just want Ned."

My mother pulled grandmother back into the room. Uncle Ned shut the door, but not before grandmother had time to recognize three men in the mob as her own half-brothers, Bob, Pink and Frank Johnson. They and she had the same father and they all knew that. When she asked them what they were doing with that mob, they said, "We just come along with the rest of the crowd."

By this time the storm was raging full force, and the mob was huddling around the side of the house out of the wind and rain. Inside the darkened room my grandfather, who was still living with us, walked back and forth, praying and mourning and asking Uncle Ned what he'd done to get these men after him like this. Grandmother explained that Ned had been working for Bold Bunch for $10 a month and wanted to quit when his time was out. Bold Bunch was framing him so as to keep from paying grandmother for the work Ned, who was 17 at the time, had done.

Meanwhile Uncle Ned was nursing an old shotgun, waiting for the mob to break down the door. But by 4 a.m., when the storm let up, they just left and went home.

After daybreak Grandmother went into the yard and there she found a live shotgun shell. We were living down behind the backwoods on Tom Glenn's place. These men could not have got to our house without coming through Glenn's yard on the highway. So, early the next morning she took the shell and went up to Glenn's. When she told him about the men coming to our log cabin, he just cursed and stomped his feet, saying they came on his land without permission, and he sure was going to find out about it.

My grandmother took Uncle Ned and my mother in her old buggy and went to Lexington, the courthouse of Oglethorpe County, taking the shotgun shell with her. She reported the threat to her son's life and limb, and they sent out the high sheriff on horseback to bring Tom Glenn back. (It was 15 miles to Glenn's place.) He was put under a peace bond and held responsible for my grandmother's family, including Uncle Ned.

That fall (1903) just after my grandmother had finished gathering in all the crops—corn, potatoes, peanuts, cotton—Tom Glenn sent the deputy sheriff down to nail up our barn doors; he had got papers claiming our hogs and cows as well as our crop. David Arnold, another landlord, went on bond for the crop and the livestock and moved us all to a house on his plantation that had been left over from slavery days. All the land around the old shack was goat pasture. For cleaning it and putting it under cultivation, Arnold gave my grandmother all she made on it for two years.

At the same time she and Tom Glenn were fighting

each other in the courts. She never missed showing up there every third Saturday, rain or shine, from 1903 to 1907, the period for which Glenn claimed her crop and livestock—though many times he himself didn't show up. In the final trial (1907) my grandmother won the case and Glenn had to pay the court costs of $30. After that the white landlords, who respected her in spite of themselves, calling her "Lawyer Julie," avoided getting into the courts with her. She couldn't even read her own name but they gave her credit for good, sound judgment.

As you can see, my grandmother had a lot of courage; today we would call her a militant. She never gave up. We would sit around the fireplace—we children along with the older people—and she would tell us that the Yankees from the North would be coming back to really set our people free.

When peddlers from the North came, with their shoulder-borne bundles of dress goods, stockings, aprons, and so forth, grandmother would talk to them about the North, and she'd tell them: "The Yankees are sure comin' back to finish the job they started." I don't remember what they answered, but we grew up thinking that all the white people up North were our friends and were ready to fight for our full emancipation when the right time came.

It was a good thing she instilled some hope into us, because Black people in our part of the country had a very hard time of it. It was a regular thing for them to be flogged at night. "Oh Lord, have mercy!" we could hear them cry through the darkness. If you were Black, you might be beaten at any time of day, when it came to that. It was common to hear the sounds of Negroes being chased through the woods by bloodhounds. We would hear the older people say, "You better be careful tonight; there's a runaway out in them woods."

The runaway might be a man trying to escape from a peonage farm or a prison-labor camp or a chain gang, but what the older folks meant by that warning was that the whites with the hounds and guns wouldn't be any too particular what Blacks they caught in their manhunt.

Such a fate just missed overtaking Royal Mattox, Aunt Georgia May's husband, at the time of Ebb Cox's lynching. Ebb lived in Wilkes County, right next to Oglethorpe County where he was lynched. The white people claimed he had killed a landlord farmer's wife, so they had taken him and tied him to an iron post. Then they heaped cordwood all around him, soaked it with gasoline and set it on fire. And all this was at high noon with the bright sun shining, which meant that what was going on must have got the say-so from the powers that be. As I heard it, the crowd of "decent white people" was so tremendous on the highway that Uncle Royal, driving home from Athens, decided to see what they were celebrating. As he came closer, he caught sight of the trussed-up man; it was like they were barbecuing some animal for a picnic.

The mob caught sight of him, while at the same time some of the people there recognized him as a neighbor. Several men grabbed him and were hollering for attention before throwing him, too, into the fire. The voices from where Uncle Royal lived finally got through. "Don't bother him. We know him."

"You-all know this nigger? You-all speak for him?"

"We know him. He's all right. Leave him alone."

They hated to have their pleasure taken away, and Uncle Royal fully expected a bullet in his back before he could drive out of range. But all he got, besides a big scare (and another lesson in what people later called race relations) was the sound of cusses and threats. One threat, he said, he didn't have any trouble obeying: "You git outta here! And you better not look back!"

Those very neighbors who had spoken up for Royal were hollering that evening when they came back from the lynching: "We got the goddam nigger! We burned the nigger! And we'll get the next one, too, if you-all don't stay in your goddam place!" We wondered whether Uncle Royal realized that the threat was aimed at him directly, and at the rest of the family, indirectly.

My grandfather was born a slave in Georgia; he was a big boy, in his early teens, when the Black people of Wilkes County got their freedom. My grandparents were poor; one-mule tenant farmers. Their mule's name was Bailey, after a white man who swapped and sold mules and horses, from whom they had bought their mule.

Grandfather was a Methodist and a kind of local preacher. He didn't have a church of his own, but sometimes he was invited into a pulpit. He was a medium-built, Black man—very black, and he could not read or write. Sometimes he would go down into the pine woods beyond our cow barn and he would preach to a bunch of trees as though they were people. Uncle Ned laughed at him; said he was preparing to preach before a church congregation. My mother would send me to call him out of the woods to come and get something to eat. I was so little at that time that I was scared I might see a snake, so I'd call out from the edge of the woods and tell him to come home.

Grandfather and Uncle Ned never got along. Actually he was my grandfather's stepson, pretty much grown up when grandmother married her second husband. Ned belonged to a newer generation, and his stepfather had come up under slavery, so the younger man must have had some trouble seeing things from the old man's viewpoint. Anyhow, the break-up between my grandparents was partly due to my Uncle Ned.

We didn't know just what kind of life my uncle lived, but the fact was that there were tales around the countryside about him and his doings, and we knew he was a pretty independent fellow. At 17 he seemed like a grown man to me.

My grandmother worried about him. Like that Sunday night, for instance, when he didn't come home from church. My grandfather was away from home at that time, working in another county. A full moon was shining that night, and my grandmother kept going to the door and looking down the dirt road to the thick, dark woods my uncle had to come through to get home. She stood in the doorway and then she called as loud as she could, "Ned! You, Ned!" When he didn't answer we were all scared; we imagined all sorts of things happening to him, and what we found out next morning was like a nightmare come true.

As soon as it was daylight, my five-foot grandmother and the rest of us trailing behind her stepped out that door and went marching down the long dirt road and through the woods and the pasture until we came to the gate at the other side near the church. We saw, scattered around, Uncle Ned's good coat, his vest and white shirt, all bloody, and grandmother cried out that Ned had been murdered.

Our neighbors, white and Black, men and women, joined our family later on that hot September day in hunting for my uncle. Well, he wasn't found then, dead or alive, but some time later that year, he was arrested in Athens, a town of around 3,000 about 30 miles away, in Clarke County. As he told it, he felt he had to get away from the neighborhood where we were living, so he started walking. He got as far as Atlanta and he didn't have enough money to buy even a sandwich, so he tried to make his way back home on foot.

We never knew what charge he was arrested for in Athens. Anyway, he was brought back to Lexington, where he was accused of jumping bond. He was tried in Lexington Courthouse and sentenced to serve twelve months on the prison cotton farm run by Big Jim Smith. Years later I learned that many Negroes who were framed in Lexington Court were sent to Smith's farm, put into prison shackles, with a ball and chain on their legs, and made to work like slaves on the chain gang farms.

To go back a bit, when Uncle Ned was arrested, he sent word to my grandmother by her pastor to bring him some clean clothes. She made up a bundle of Ned's clothes and told my grandfather about it when he got home that night. He became very angry and told her if she wanted Ned to have any clothes carried to him she would have to carry them herself, because he sure wasn't going to Lexington for them white folks up there to put him in jail. My grandparents then had a big battle of words, which ended up with his packing his trunk, putting it on his back and leaving home. They had been at the breaking point ever since my grandmother had taken us home to live with her. When he left us that night, in the fall of 1903, it was for good.

We moved to Dave Arnold's place, and after Uncle Ned had served his 12 months slaving in Big Jim's cotton fields, he came back home. But he spent that first year working in Elberton for a Black landlord who beat his field hands as if he owned them. In the early spring of 1905, Ned started to help my grandmother make the crop for that year, working at the same time on land that belonged to a farmer named Sam Hubbard.

I used to get a good feeling out there, sometimes, picking cotton along with Uncle Ned and his friends (some of whom he had perhaps met in prison) who stopped by and joined us. They would be talking and joshing and laughing while they picked cotton, and I would forget how my back was hurting. Because bending over in the hot sun, hour after hour, dragging that heavy bag of cotton with the loop over my shoulder cutting into it—that could be a living hell for a person suffering from a weak back or for little children.

So when Uncle Ned's friends would tell their tall tales

about all the places they'd been to, and how the driving wheels of the great big locomotives were made of pasteboard, that would be fun. I used to wonder if the day would ever come when I would even get near a locomotive, let alone ride in a coach next to one.

In 1906 we moved from Arnold's place to a farm owned by a man named Jones, where, just as we had at the other places, we stayed one year, made one crop and moved on. When I was nine, we set out for a big plantation over in Wilkes County, where I learned to plow. Uncle Ned was living with us but working for a Negro farmer, Dave Huff. It was at that time that my Aunt Georgia May and I became the regular plowhands on whom grandmother depended altogether.

The way it was with sharecropping was this: First the landlord would furnish us families with the most rundown, poorest land with rocky soil and ditches cut crisscross every which way by rain water rushing from the high ground. Before we could begin to work the land, we had to lay branches of pine saplings in the ditches. In time, this acted like a brake on the flooding waters, and the heavy rainfalls would then partly fill the ditches with soil. But though all this work helped to keep the soil from being washed away, it didn't make it any richer. It still needed fertilizer, and that cost money.

After we had planted and raised the crop, the landlord enjoyed the right to take not only our share of the cotton but also the cotton seeds, if he thought we owed him more than enough—according to his accounting. We owed him for fertilizer and for food. So far as the food was concerned, which was a guarantee that we would make the crop, it would usually be cut off around the first or second week in July, about the time we were laying the crop by. From then until we picked enough cotton to make at least one bale, we'd have to do the best we could for food.

When the first bale was ginned (that is, when the seed had been combed out of the fiber) and we sold both the cotton and the seed, we had to take half of the money we got and apply it on the debt and keep half for food.

This was the way it was with Dr. Rayles, in 1909; at Jim Algood's in 1910; at Jake Elbahard's in 1911; and with Willie Pollion, a Negro four-mule landlord, in 1912. William Pollion did what Tom Glenn could not do to us in 1903—when we had picked about 800 pounds of his cotton during the last week of August, he claimed the whole crop, including the sweet potatoes and peanuts we raised for home use.

We moved that year, on the first of September, to the home of a Negro farmer named Man Wallace. We went out from there and picked cotton by the hundred pounds for different farmers. In this way we were able to make money enough to buy food and shoes and a few clothes for the winter of 1912.

There were many times before we laid the crop by when we wouldn't have anything to eat except the vegetables we raised in our garden—cabbage, collard greens, maybe some cucumbers and tomatoes, and almost always some okra and turnips—but no fats, no meat to cook with the vegetables. Often we didn't have bread. My grandmother would go out and break ears of corn off the stalks when it wasn't dry enough to take to the mill for grinding and yet too hard to be boiled or roasted. She would flatten out a tin can into one long strip and take a hammer and nails and punch holes in that piece of metal. Then she'd grate the corn, making it into something like grits; mix it with water and a little salt and we'd eat it in place of bread.

And all the while, no matter how hard we worked, there was the atmosphere of threat and intimidation all around us. As children we didn't have to see things with our own eyes to know what was going on—any more than one has to see the air in order to breathe it. There were constant stories and rumors of beatings and killings and nightriders. And some came mighty close to home, like what happened to Uncle Mose when he was about 50.

Uncle Mose lived with his deaf wife on a farm seven miles or so away from us. Right next to their shack 50 acres belonged to a white man, Bell; on the other side, another white man, Leck Glenn, lived. Bell, it was said, was in debt, and after he tried to sell his 50 acres to Glenn and the deal fell through, he turned around and offered the tract to Uncle Mose. So Uncle bought the land, which was right on the highway.

When the land was surveyed, it turned out that his line took in Glenn's barn. Glenn said he would move it, but Uncle Mose said, "I don't have to have that small bit of land. Just let it stay there."

Uncle Mose had two fine mules. He had laid his crop by for some weeks, and everything looked fine—three ears of corn, some big as a man's forearm, on every one of those stalks. And that cotton! From the highest branches down to those close to the ground, it had dozens of open bolls like big white roses mixed in among the dark green leaves. This part of the cotton the farmers called the first crop.

From the waist up to near the top, the bolls were not full-grown yet. The blossoms were still on the bolls; this part of the bush would yield the *middle* or second picking, and then the *top* picking, which was a long way from being developed, would begin, say, around late November.

Now it was September and out there in the wide spaces of his new farm and his rich crop, Uncle Mose was picking cotton. His thoughts must have been about all the things a 50-year-old Black farmer's life was made up of—how many bales each picking would yield; how much each 500-pound bale would bring in solid cash, and so forth. And perhaps he was thinking about his wife, who was not too well and increasingly deaf.

In any case, one of those needlepointed ends of a dried cotton boll suddenly jabbed the tip of his finger. As his finger bled profusely and gave him agonizing pain, he decided to go and ask someone at Glenn's for some spirits of turpentine, which was what many people used for cuts and bruises those days. As he came near the house, he saw a white woman watching him. She stood on the porch, staring at him. Uncle Mose stopped, took off his hat and said, "Please, ma'am, may I have a little turpentine for my hurt finger?"

"Wait there," she said, "and I'll get you some."

He stood there waiting for the turpentine, and when she came out of the house he saw she had a shotgun pointing at him. He could not make her understand he meant no harm. And he couldn't go on standing there at the edge of her yard talking to a white woman, let alone arguing with her. She became more and more agitated, and her voice grew louder and louder until he left her yard.

Not long after, a mob of white men with bloodhounds chased Uncle Mose through the woods and over to the neighboring county. One story we were told said they caught up with him and put him on a chain gang for a year; some said they lynched him. One thing was sure: everybody knew that he never did harvest his fine crop of cotton and corn, because it rotted in the field on that 50 acres of rich land adjoining his good neighbor, Mr. Glenn. Back in those days white people in the county just didn't want a Black man owning land next to theirs—and right on the main highway.

I was about 15 then and I still thought that the Yankees would be coming back from up North to finish freeing us. Some years later, plowing in the fields all by myself, with lots of time to daydream, I would imagine how it would be to get a bunch of men together and meet a lynch mob face-to-face and break it up. I would be following the old mule, doing my plowing, and I would wonder why grown folks were so afraid to take action.

And then I would remember how it was when my grandmother used to go off to Lexington to the county courthouse, and how she'd leave me and my brother with a neighbor, Mary Thornton, and we would sleep on the floor with just a thin quilt or some rags over us. I would remember the talk about the mad dogs out there in the dark and the wolves waiting in the woods, and the shotguns the white men carried. And then I knew that I, too, would be scared and might never be big and strong enough to confront the all-powerful white man.

2

SHARECROPPERS ARE ALWAYS MOVING

Like other Negro sharecroppers, we were always moving, always in the hope of finding a landlord who would not take advantage of us. But we hardly ever succeeded in bettering our condition.

In 1909, a year after my Aunt Georgia May got married, Uncle Ned came home and took over the handling of our farm. He did that for only one year, however, and then decided to quit the countryside and get a job at the railroad station in Burklin, Georgia. He never did come back to live with us.

In 1913 we moved to the farm of Bob Johnson, one of my grandmother's three white half-brothers, whom I mentioned as being a part of the mob that came to lynch my Uncle Ned some ten years earlier. Grandmother told us how Bob Johnson was always keeping after her to come to live on his place—as if he was trying to make up for that night. When we finally moved to his place, where he owned a sawmill, I was 15 years old.

How did we get along—this big, red-faced, reddish-haired white man, actually my granduncle, and his Black oppressed relatives? Bob and his wife Cynthia had five children, one boy and three girls older than I, who never paid me any mind at all, and a boy about my age, who played with me.

It was my job in the sawmill to keep the falling sawdust back from under the saw when it cut through the green pine logs. When the mill wasn't running, I had to help the rest of the millhands to stack the new-cut lumber, moving it back from the mill to make way for the green logs that were always coming in.

Bob Johnson didn't pay me for my work at the sawmill, though he had promised me 50 cents a day for working from sunup to sundown. He would give my grandmother a certain amount of food, such as home-cured meat from his smokehouse, vegetables from his garden and corn meal. He had a large patch of winter turnips—"rutabag-ers," we used to call them—and every so often his wife would give my grandmother a small amount for a meal.

While we worked on the farm making the crop, Bob would issue my grandmother her weekly supply of food, and that went on until we laid the crop by late in July, when he stopped feeding us. Grandmother wouldn't allow me to work any more at the sawmill for nothing. We managed somehow to make it until cotton-picking time, when she sold Bob Johnson her half of the cotton-seed from the first bale. Then we bought some food and were able to gather the rest of our crop.

A bale of cotton in those days had to weigh around 500 pounds, after the seeds had been removed. We made six bales that year and we sold our cotton at 15 cents a pound. We were able to settle our debts with Bob Johnson for the food and the fertilizer he had advanced us. We cleared $75 or $80 but he couldn't pay us all the money when settlement day came. He said to my grandmother in his house that night, "We be half brother and half sister, but you don't want me to have nothing. Yes, I owe you some more money, but I ain't going to give it to you."

She said, "All right, you taking that, but you won't be able to take no more. I'm leaving here and I hope we don't meet again, in hell or heaven."

At just about this time, when we were moving from Bob Johnson's farm to Jones Collins' farm in the same county, we got word about my grandfather dying. I was in charge of our family now. I was 16 years old and near six foot tall, about the age my Uncle Ned was when my grandmother and grandfather broke up for the last time, in 1903. We lived with Jones Collins through 1916, and in 1917 we moved to Taylor Hall's. That was the year I got married, at the age of 19, to Lucy Goosby.

Early in 1918, Lucy and I began to sharecrop for one year with Taylor Hall, while my grandmother took my brother to my mother and stepfather. I bought a mule from Taylor Hall for $316, paying him in 1,000 pounds of ginned cotton rent for the land for each year. For the next five years that was my payment for the use of the land. Lucy and I made some very good crops up through 1920, and then the boll weevil began to ruin the cotton and the budworms ruined the corn, no matter how we fought the pests. I gave up trying to farm in the fall of 1922.

In 1923 I went to work for Tom Jackson at $10 a month. Each week was five-and-a-half days. Each workday started at sunup and ended at sundown. At the end of seven months with Jackson, I'd had enough of wage-working, and you'll see why when I tell you of my experiences on that farm. They had a whole lot to do with shaping my thinking the way it is today.

Mr. Jackson, to begin with, was a great believer in God and God's word, the Holy Bible. He was one of the big head-deacons of the white folks' Baptist Church in that community. What first puzzled me about this church was that right in front of this holy building, in that beautiful yard of spotless white sand on the main highway, stood the remains of the old slave block, about five feet high and six feet square, carved out of Georgia's famous blue granite (the kind beautiful tombstones are made of). Many old people, born in slavery days, remembering all the horrors of their early years, would see that granite block and, in their minds' eyes, still see their loved ones being sold from it.

At the time I contracted to work for Jackson at $10 a month, plus one bushel of white cornmeal and ten pounds of white slab salt pork, we had a four-year-old son. And that was absolutely all the pay I got for a month's work. At the end of each month I would ask Mr. Jackson to figure my bill for what I had bought from his grocery store—things like shortening, a can of salmon, a can of tripe so we could have a bit of luxury for the weekend. I was watching close, determined to stay out of his debt, so when I asked him to figure how much I owed him at the end of each month and it always added up to 20 or 30 cents, I began to be worried.

While trying to think of some way to keep from being absolutely clamped into his trap, I kept working, not talking about it to the other fellows. Mr. Tom Jackson was looked upon by most of the Blacks and poor whites as a wonderful man. That wasn't only because he had a 25-mule plantation of cotton and corn and lived in a large white colonial house built in slavery days by unpaid Black labor. He was also the father of a big family of handsome boys and pretty daughters; he had a cotton gin and a grist mill: the first, to gin and bale everybody's cotton; the second, to grind everybody's corn. He owned a sawmill; was the owner or part owner of three stores—a grocery at the home place, another one about two-and-a-half miles away at Cross Roads, and a drygoods store in Tignell, about ten miles down the road—and, in addition, he was Justice of the Peace.

Mr. Jackson was also a Christian gentleman. He would not allow himself or anybody else to put a hand to a hoe, an ax or a plow until he had turned to the Psalms in his Bible and read from them, while we all stood in silence with heads bowed.

One morning Uncle Pate Cade—we all called him Uncle Pate—who was along in years (he had spent his early life in slavery) asked Mr. Jackson, "Old Boss, let me pray this morning." Old Boss said, "No, Pate, I rather not. You let me do the praying." And everybody laughed. But I said to myself, "Is this God Mr. Jackson is serving a different God from the one Negroes pray to?"

Out in the field with the other plowhands, I raised questions about the small wages we were making. Mr. Jackson paid Walter Wall, his top Negro, $15 a month. My wages were $10; Frank Huff, who was 17 years old, was paid $7.50 a month, though he worked from sunup to sundown, five-and-a-half days a week.

"How is it," I would ask, "that Mr. Jackson believes so much in God that he don't want us to do anything until he reads the Bible, and yet he don't pay us more for these long hours out here in the hot sun?"

They would come up with all kinds of answers. Like, for instance, that Mr. Jackson was getting his reward now, but God sees all things and we would get ours at the end of this life.

We would argue back and forth, but it never changed the fact that I was averaging about 33 cents for a 16-hour day, and by the middle of May I still hadn't saved any money in spite of all my efforts. Then one day I got what I considered a real bright idea. I had been attending church services every Sunday and I decided to ask among the farmers who attended which of them had peanuts left over after the planting. I bought them from both Black and white farmers for $2 a bushel and took them home. Then I removed the rack from our little four-eyed, woodburning cook stove, made a blazing hot fire and put a peck of peanuts at a time in the oven.

As the peanuts were parched or, as people say nowadays, roasted, I put them in a large flax bag. I would do this on Friday night and early Saturday afternoon. Then I took a salmon can, polished it up, and after putting a strap on each end of the bag to carry it by, I would go late Saturday afternoon to where the farmers and farm workers hung out at Jackson's grocery store. I sold my big bag of parched peanuts at five cents a can.

On Sunday I went to the church and took my stand down at the spring where the people came to get a fresh drink of cool water. There I sold my peanuts every Sunday, from the middle of May until the first week in August (this was in 1923), and when my seven months were up at the end of July and Mr. Jackson went over my account and I was in debt 13 cents, I dug down into my pocket and came up with a handful of change. I counted out exactly two nickels and three pennies and handed them to him. The total amount of money my wife Lucy and I had saved from selling peanuts was a little more than $40.

We had been planning that I should go to Atlanta, and that when I got settled in a good job I would send for her and our child. That is how I finally broke out of the trap on the plantation of that Christian gentleman, Tom Jackson. I left Lucy and little Hosea with my father-in-law, Zack Goosby, and his wife Jessie, and I headed for Atlanta.

3

PLOWHAND INTO
INDUSTRIAL WORKER

I used to pray to be able to get a job where I could earn
a decent wage and work decent hours. I thought it would
be wonderful to be paid the tremendous sum of $5 a day
which, I was told, a young, strong man could earn in
Atlanta, Ga.

I didn't have any trouble getting a common laborer's
job in the Nashville, Chattanooga and St. Louis Railroad
shop. They told me I would be paid 30 cents an hour for a
seven-day week, but they didn't tell me how many hours
I would have to put in each day. I found that out for
myself.

My job was in and around the coal chute. You could lay
off on any day except Sunday. If you made Sunday your
day off, you were automatically fired, so I began by being
very careful to remember that Sunday was not going to
be any day of rest for me, even though I had been taught
that it was a sin to work on Sunday. Later on I figured
out that "six days shalt thou labor and do all thy work"
means that you should rest on *any* one of the seven days
so you could have strength to work on the other six.

There were three of us working around the coal chute,
all of us Black men. We had to fill the chute, which was a
90-foot-high wooden structure straddling two railroad
tracks, one side holding five carloads of coal and the
other side, four carloads. Beginning at 7 o'clock in the
morning and working until 11 at night some days, our
job was to fill up that chute with coal from the open cars.
There wasn't any extra-time pay, just straight 30 cents

an hour, and it never stormed so furiously nor rained too hard, nor did the sun ever shine too hot nor cold winds whip around us too roughly for us to fill up that coal chute. Picking chunks out of those frozen coal cars was just like picking at stone from the side of a mountain of hard rock.

Around 2:30 p.m. the switch engine was brought out of the roundhouse by the hostler and his helper to be coaled up for the switchman, who had to begin his job switching cars out on to the terminal yard. We would get up on the tender of each one of the engines—I remember hearing people say the tender was the engine's lunchbox and thermos bottle—and we measured the coal with a long steel rod, after which we took our shovels and leveled the coal off even. Then we would tell the straw boss on the ground what number the coal measured up to on the steel rod.

When my Uncle Ned's friend, who was picking cotton along with us, used to tell us that the big driving wheels of the locomotives were made out of pasteboard, I had no way of knowing if he was telling the truth; we children didn't think our grown folks would lie, especially to kids. So when I went to work at the railroad shops I didn't ask anybody what those wheels were made of; I was looking for a chance to find out for myself.

One day the roundhouse foreman took me from the coal chute to help the spring-gang mechanic "shrink the tires" on the driving wheels of one of the old steam engines. And this is how we shrank those "pasteboard" driving wheels with oil, air and fire:

First, we jacked up the wheels clear off the tracks. Then the mechanic took his gauge and evened up the rims of the wheels, and we took parts of thin sheets of metal and placed them even, all around the wheel between the tire and the rim. After that we placed a coil of pipe about half an inch thick, with tiny holes on the inner side, next to the rim. At one end of the pipe there was a coupling for another pipe (to be connected); at the other end the pipe was coupled to a rubber hose, which was connected to a 15-gallon oil tank mounted on two wheels. A pipe on the other side of the tank was connected to an air hose. We then put small scraps of rag waste between the coil of pipe and the tire, stuck a lighted match to the rags—after which we turned on the air hose. On the other side of the oil tank, as the air began to blow oil through the tiny holes in the coiled pipe, the steel rim got cherry-red hot, so we cut off the air hose, pulled the coiled pipe off the rim of the driving wheel and turned on the hose pipe of cold water. When the steel rim was cooled, it was welded solid onto that wheel.

And that was how I found out what locomotive wheels were really made of.

On many occasions, after that job with the spring-gang, the roundhouse foreman would come to the coal chute and arrange with the straw boss for me to work for some of the mechanics, who were all white, while their helpers were all Black. A mechanic and his helper, working in close quarters side by side, day after day, month after month, got to know each other's dispositions pretty well. The Black man, dependent on the white mechanic for a chance to make a living, is likely to fall in with the mechanic's disposition or his way of doing things or looking at life.

Since I was six-foot tall and muscular, I got to be called on more and more when one of the mechanic's regular helpers was down sick, or when they had some extra-heavy lifting to do in the roundhouse. When I worked a full day doing a helper's job, I got a helper's pay, $4.68 for an eight-hour day; if I worked only a few hours every day of the week as a helper, I only got the laborer's pay, 30 cents an hour. Sometimes I worked a couple of days before they sent me back to the coal chute. I was not the only one who noticed that whenever an opening came up for a full-time helper, the company master mechanic would hire a new man.

On November 1, 1924, I went to the master mechanic and told him I wanted all my time. He asked what was the matter. Why did I want to quit my job on the coal chute? I told him I was leaving town and going to Birmingham. "If you weren't quitting, I was planning to put you to helping," he said. I told him thanks but I had made my plans to be in Birmingham the next week. I could have told him that I had heard of a Negro earning $5 a day in Birmingham. But I didn't because it had turned out to be too good to be true in Georgia and it could turn out the same way in Alabama.

I didn't have any trouble getting a job at the Stockham Pipe and Fittings plant just outside of Birmingham. And the first thing I learned—after I found that my workday was from six in the morning to six at night—was that I was paid only according to the number of perfect iron molds I produced. No wages at all if I didn't make any molds in a given week, no matter how hard I worked and how much time I put in trying to learn. If I had to learn, some molds would have to be spoiled.

The idea of working in a place where a metal as solid as iron could be melted down to run like water and look like a stream of fire had a kind of stunning effect on me. My foreman took charge of teaching me how to mold iron, beginning with a 4-inch Tee—a pipe joint shaped like the letter *T*. Making molds was a hot and muscle-wearying job, but it was also a highly skilled job in my opinion—the worker must concentrate all his thoughts because molding is not a set pattern of acts, one right after the other. Castings cannot all be made the same way and in the same temper of sand.

The whole interior of the place was hot as the living hell. Most of us would have on just a pair of overalls or some old hip pants; we didn't wear shirts. The water in the drinking pipes at the time was hot enough to take a bath in, and the men were always thirsty for a drink of cool water.

Some of the men would get 20 and 40 gallon barrels and put 100 pounds of ice in each of them, filling them with water; then they would charge everybody 15 cents a week. There were many of us, with sweat running off our half-naked bodies like rain, who didn't seem to know how to stop drinking, once we started. We'd just stand there gulping down that cold, refreshing water, and the next thing we'd know there'd be a fellow or two knocked out with cramps. There was always a stretcher in the box beside the wall, and when a man fell out, a couple of guys ran and got the stretcher, put him on it and hurried him on to the so-called doctor's office. From there they would rush him to the company's hospital. Sometimes, we would get the news the next day that Jim or Big Red or Shorty or Slim was dead.

The company's responsibility—besides furnishing the stretchers—was $500 for the family if the worker died; if he lived and was out two weeks or more, they paid him $9 a week up to nine weeks.

When I went into the Stockham Pipe and Fitting foundry in November 1924, I heard that 1,800 molders were working there and that most of them were Black. There were some whites working on the big box flares, side by side with Negroes. The Black were being paid 50 cents an hour and the whites $1.25: $10 a day to white workers, $4 a day to Black workers.

The bulk of Negro common labor was to be found in the wage brackets of 27 to 32 cents an hour in steel plants and in small and large foundries and shops. There were superintendents and assistant-supers in the various departments; in the plants some companies had a super in each department with three assistants and under these assistants there would be the "little" boss, the straw boss, of groups of workers, who would turn the time in for the men under him and also told them what time to report for work.

If the regular time was 7 o'clock, the little boss would tell his men to come in at 4:30 or 5 and these workers often stayed on the job straight through until 6:30 or 7, or even later at night. The regular working time was supposed to be from 7 a.m. to 3 or 3:30 p.m. and the white workers—with a few exceptions—would always start and stop by the official time. But then they were in the skilled and semi-skilled brackets.

On a Friday or Saturday payday when Negro workers went up to the pay window to get their checks, they would in most cases find themselves many hours short in each week's pay. When they told the pay boss at the window how much time they had put in, he would say, "You-all have to see the foreman you work for." And when they looked for their foreman, somebody would call out, "He done went home." But even when they found the straw boss in the shop, now it was his turn to pass the buck. "Wait till Monday," he would tell them, "and I'll get your time straightened out."

Even after this run-around, the workers still had a faint hope they would be paid the balance of their wages on Monday, the day they had promised the grocery man, the furniture man, the rent man, or the insurance-policy man he would get his money. But no such thing; on Monday morning the straw boss told the workers he would see about their time later in the day when he had a chance to go up to the office. Then came the alibis: "Your time got lost and the timekeeper couldn't find it"; or, "Your time will be on your pay slip this coming payday"; or, "I forgot to check with the timekeeper and he's out of the office and won't be back today." The straw boss's answer to the Black worker's complaints depended on how much he liked his looks; how much that worker bowed and pulled off his hat and generally played Uncle Tom. Some of us just couldn't put on that kind of act.

Most of the Negroes—if they were not what was called common day laborers—were box-flare molders and snap-floor molders making tees, ells, Y's and so on—all the different kinds of fittings or joints. They ranged in size from one inch to four feet in diameter, measured on the inside. All the fittings called for different degrees of wetness or dryness in the sand used to make the molds; some of the sand had to be wet or heavy; some had to be drier or light. If the sand was too wet, the mold that was made of it would reject the liquid iron, the soupy metal would boil out of the "gate"—the opening in the mold. On the other hand, if the metal was too cold it wouldn't make the fitting because the liquid iron would slow down and stop running into the gate of the mold before the fitting was completely formed. If the sand wasn't moist enough when the hot metal was poured into the gate, the dry sand would wash into the mold, and then the fitting would become scrap iron. Even if the liquid metal was hot enough to run like water, it still wouldn't be hot enough to "burn up" that loose sand.

So these many different fittings had to be made with many different degrees of temper of sand. The sand we used was not just one grade. First, there was the kind we molders left on the floor. But the hot metal soon burned all the strength out of it. In order to keep it strong enough to make the casting, we would have to add new grades of sand to sustain the strength of the old. Some of the fittings required strong sand and closed; others, strong sand and open. The molder had to be skilled enough to know this by squeezing a handful of sand to make sure it was right for a particular mold.

My foreman kept telling me he was paying me by the piece, bringing out the sheet every Tuesday or Wednesday and pasting it on the board. It told how much money we had earned and how many molds we had lost. I would look at my name and read: $2.90 . . . $2.90 . . . " I figured it came to 15 cents a mold. Though I had put out 30 or 40 molds every day, I still had just $2.90.

And there was always this little straw boss. If he didn't like the way you dressed, or thought you smoked cigars too often, or took exception to your tone of voice or what you said (or maybe to the fact that you hardly said anything) you would have a hard way to go on your job. Once you and your little boss fell out, it was ten-to-one you wouldn't make it with the rest of them. When a Black man really put up a fight for his rights—say, the right to act like a man where that was called for or to draw a man's wage for a man's job—they would say that "nigra" was crazy. And a "crazy nigra" was so dangerous that any white man had the right and the duty to protect society from him. If the Black man was a hard and productive worker, that is, if he put in full time and turned out good work even though he was "crazy" the super would tell the straw boss, "If you and that nigra can't agree, don't you bother him. You just send him to me."

The big super would shift this worker to another crew under a different straw boss. In most cases you could make it all right, at least for a while, with this new straw, because the super wanted you to produce. The little boss knew that you wouldn't stand for being pushed around, so it was best for him if he let things be. On the other hand, it was always best for you to take the long way home, because once you got fired it wasn't much use to head toward the next gate. You'd be turned away when you got there.

I began to worry about my wife and kid who stayed in Atlanta till they could join me in Birmingham, where I went to earn $5 a day. Yet the way things were now, I had to stay in Birmingham; I certainly couldn't go back to the railroad job in Atlanta. Eventually I was able to send for my family and I had one less worry on my mind. But my big worry now was how to make enough money to keep a roof over our heads and have food and clothes.

I worked that whole first year as an extra man, without a floor. What I mean by this is: each molder had a space about 12 by 12 foot—that was his floor. He had his machine and his sand on a 12-foot square space that would hold from 75 to 100 finished molds, depending on their size. That many molds would come to about $5 worth of work—maybe even $6. Those molders we called "road-men" could put up 100 to 105 molds a day at 11 cents and could earn $10 a day. But they were over-average men or it was a speed-up and I didn't work that fast.

I managed that first year to pay my rent and my insurance policies and dues in the church, because I had learned how to make up to $5 a day sometimes. But the big IF was always there dogging my steps. If the metal got too cold, or if all my castings were bad, or if my sand was too wet or dry, and so forth, my day's work might turn out "scrap" and I wouldn't get any pay.

And if they lost three or four castings in the tapping room it was not the tapping room that stood the loss—it was Hosea Hudson. Say, I made 45 molds and all of them landed on the scrap pile. When the sheet went up I see that I got $2.50 or $2.75 coming to me, though I actually turned out $4.50 worth of work. So I'd have to go to the office and they would tell me so and so many pieces "got lost" in the shipping room.

Gradually, as the years passed, my position as a

worker, my status as a molder, improved. In what they called the gray-iron department, on the first floor, I was among the few molders they came to with jobs that even some of the old-timers could not make. It got so that I never turned down a job because it was too difficult; I had complete confidence that I could handle it.

In 1929 the department foreman came to me one day and asked me whether I would try a job out. I didn't have a molding job on at the time—this was during the depression—and I was doing day work up and down the gang cleaning up scrap iron.

I asked, "What are you going to do with the two fellows on that job now?"

"I'm going to put them in the gangway."

I said, "All right, I'll try it to help you out and to see if I can make it."

When he asked me who I wanted to make cores for me, I said, "Tee Ferguson," a fellow who had been in the gang doing day work along with me. Tee was at the foundry when I first went to work there; he was older than I and a very nice guy.

The day we started to work as a team, the two fellows whom we were replacing had put out 290 molds with four castings to the mold, and they had 190 castings in scraps. I asked the foreman: "How long are you going to give me to try out?" and he said, "Oh, two or three weeks."

I showed Tee how I wanted him to make the core—he was a more experienced molder than I. I said we would just take our time; we couldn't rush. Because he was older than I, he was more scared about losing his job, inclined to overdo it at the sight of the foreman. So I told him we would experiment on the job to see what we could do.

The day after those other two men had put out 290 molds, we put out 250. They had 190 castings in scrap; we had six. I told Tee, "Man, we got it! You just make your cores like I showed you and I'm going to make the coke and drag off the mold the same, too."

In 1930 that job was paying us four cents a mold—$4 for 100 molds. We put up from 325 to 350 a day. In the meantime, the depression was deepening—so much so that in 1931 the boss started coming round and talking about cutting the prices on all the jobs. Where jobs paid three cents a mold, they wanted to cut them to 2 1/2 cents.

I said to him, "This is a hard job to make. You oughtn't to cut the pay."

He said, "I'll see. I'll let you know."

Well, he kept his word: not only did he go on to see; he sure did let us know. The job stayed four cents a mold till he took it off the ground floor and put it on the conveyor.

Under the new setup, instead of a man having to pour the liquid metal, rap out the castings, wet the hot sand, stack his boards and so on, two men worked together molding, another one poured the metal; and a fourth shook out the molds. The number of molds jumped from 50 to 100 per man per day to 250 to 450 a day, when we began the conveyor system with the two-man team turning 200 molds a day at 30 cents an hour for each man for an 8-hour day.

Naturally, wages didn't go hand in hand with the speed-up in production. If that had happened, workers wouldn't have had so many grievances and wouldn't have been mad about something most of the time. Heaped on top of the complaints in the shop was the extra burden the Black workers had to shoulder in the communities where we had to live. The time was ripe for organizations to rise up and struggle against oppressive conditions as well as the persecutions and legal lynchings of innocent Black men— as typified in the Scottsboro Case.

4

LEGAL LYNCHINGS

As the depression continued, my education in the hardships and injustices inflicted on the working class —and especially on the Black workers—developed rapidly. Nineteen thirty-one was also a year in which Blacks suffered murderous treatment at the hands of Southern "justice." To millions here and abroad the name "Scottsboro" became another word for racist inhumanity. The trials, retrials, appeals, and ordeals of these nine youths lasted, all in all, through nineteen years, in spite of campaigns that aroused the conscience of the world.

So much has been written about the case that I will only touch on a few highlights here. The first newspaper accounts said, "nine Negro and three white boys had been taken off a 49-car freight train at Paint Rock, Alabama, and held for vagrancy." The Negroes ranged in age from 12 to 19, and had got into a fight with the white boys. At a stop along the way someone had phoned ahead to the sheriff at Paint Rock that the Negroes were attacking the white boys.

When the freight got to Paint Rock, the sheriff and his deputies and an excited crowd, mostly whites, were waiting. It seemed that the Black youths were going to be beat up for daring to strike white boys, but, according to regulations, they all would have to be searched first. The three white boys were dressed in overalls, and two of them turned out to be girls. The fact changed a simple vagrancy charge to one of the most vicious and long-drawn-out persecutions of Negroes in U.S. history.

By the time they reached the little town of Scottsboro, they managed to get one of the girls to say that she and her companion had been savagely raped by the Negroes. Within the hour a sullen mob had gathered, ready for a mass lynching, prevented only by the intervention of the Alabama National Guard. Before adequate legal defense was available, the youths were summarily tried, and eight were sentenced to death.

As word of the crime against justice began to reach the North, other organizations and lawyers entered the case. At an early stage the International Labor Defense, headed by William L. Patterson, enlisted with all its strength to prove the charges were a frame-up from beginning to end. The evidence of an examining physician had proved that the girls, who were prostitutes, could not have been "raped" in the time interval claimed. For ten years famous lawyers like Samuel Leibowitz, Joseph Brodsky, and George W. Chalmers were involved in one degree or another.

The NAACP had entered the defense but their antagonism to the "Communist" ILD prevented any kind of unity, and the main burden of steering the boys through one trial after another fell to the ILD.

Meanwhile a great campaign to enlist world protest was sparked by the Communist Party. The tremendous pressure of world opinion, together with the able legal efforts, saved the lives of the boys again and again. Nevertheless, for 19 years all or most of them suffered the most inhuman treatment in Southern prisons, robbed of their youth, their freedom, their right to live out their lives.

Another case that shook the Black community was that of the Williams sisters. These were two white sisters who, it was said, were on a day's outing with a girl friend in the Shades Mountain area of Birmingham. A Negro with a pistol, said the Birmingham papers, jumped on the running board of their car and ordered them to drive to a lonely spot along the Shades Mountain Valley. He kept them there for hours, the account went on, and finally, when darkness thickened in the bushes and the trees and it got harder to "control" the women, he shot them.

Two of them died; the sister that got away was supposed to have told the newspaper that this "Negro rapist-murderer" was handsome—a word a white Southern woman wouldn't use about a Black man in public, especially to a white man, regardless of what her private opinion might be. He was brown-skinned, she said, and had black, wavy (or curly) hair, was clean, wore a polka dot shirt and spoke good English.

We Blacks of Birmingham knew that night that a hunt was on for one of us in the mountain area, and that all the railroads in the section were being watched for any male Blacks trying to catch a train. Naturally, many unemployed—some with maybe a dollar or two left; some with the last penny to their names—tried to buy tickets to Atlanta or Columbus, Georgia, or Chattanooga. Many Black "hoboes," we found later, were shot and killed on the freight trains by gangs of so-called law-enforcement officers. Many of the police knew these "officers" were Ku Kluxers or members of other white-supremacist gangs. And although the community of Irondale was itself terrorized by the wholesale arrests and jailings that went on in Birmingham, not one of the hundreds of Black men came within ten miles of looking like that newspaper description.

At one point I thought the authorities were going to settle for blaming a Communist. I wasn't a member of the Party but I had watched its work and I had been listening to a young Black man named Angelo Herndon, who was in Birmingham with some friends at that time and who was said to be a Communist. (This was before he was arrested in Atlanta for leading an unemployed demonstration.) The newspapers shifted their attack from the Black community as a whole to "Negro Communists" in that community.

Just about this time, the newspapers reported that the young Williams woman and her brother were driving along a Birmingham street when suddenly she cried out, "There he is! He's the one that shot us!"

They stopped their car, called the young man over and asked his name. "Willie Peterson," he answered. Where had he been? He said he was coming from his doctor's. The newspapers said that this man was skinny; you got the impression that he was sick-looking. He in no way fitted the description the woman had given on the night of the manhunt; it was as if she had forgotten what she had said about that handsome, brown-skinned man with curly black hair. So she "identified" Peterson as the assailant-murderer, and he was arrested and lodged in Birmingham's Big Rock jail "for safekeeping."

It was there that Willie Peterson was shot by Dent Williams, the girl's brother, while the sheriff of Jefferson County was right there looking on, as was the prosecutor who was questioning Peterson.

It was a criminal offence to take arms into that jail; every visitor was supposed to be searched. But it was not Dent Williams who was put on trial; it was Willie Peterson, as soon as he had recovered a little from the gunshot wound. The ILD got Mrs. Peterson's agreement to represent her husband but certain Birmingham "Negro leaders" saw her and persuaded her that "those reds" didn't mean her any good.

Although the ILD withdrew from the defense out of consideration for Mrs. Peterson, it carried on an active campaign outside the courthouse while the NAACP carried on the legal defense. Witnesses, white and black, in the face of Klan threats testified that the defendant was at home sick on the day the women were shot on

Shades Mountain. His doctor had records of a trip he
made to Peterson's home that day. A white woman
neighbor told the all-white jury that she took fresh milk
to the Petersons that day and that he was sick in bed.
Nevertheless, the jury found him guilty, and he was
sentenced first to death, and finally to life in prison,
where he died years later.

In the same year, 1931, down around Camp Hill,
Alabama, Black sharecroppers and tenant farmers were
beginning to build the Sharecroppers Union, under the
leadership of the Communist Party. I didn't know this
till I joined the Party later that year.

For cotton-chopping, the landlords were paying from
40 to 50 cents a day, sunup to sundown, to grown men
and women—the same wage my mother and grandmother and other Black adults earned when I was a kid
on a farm in Georgia. I was many years older now, with a
wife and son of my own, no longer imagining $5 a day in
industry was a big wage. Yet there were young Black
six-footers like me in Georgia, Alabama and other areas
of the old Confederacy, just as strong and healthy and
intelligent as I was, still chopping cotton for 40 or 50
cents a day.

One night in April some of these Black farmers were
holding a meeting in one of the churches, when a few of
the big landlords and the high sheriff at Camp Hill
organized a mob and headed down there. On their way,
they spotted a watchman or guard, Ralph Gray, standing
a short distance from the church and holding a shotgun.
They fired on him. Gray returned the fire, wounding one
or two members of the mob.

Gray managed to get away and make it back to his
home. By that time, his friends and neighbors at the
scene, who were involved in the Sharecroppers Union
struggle, had gathered at Gray's home to protect him

from the mob that night. It was reported that the men
put the women in the house to look after Ralph. The
armed men organized themselves into groups and hid in
the dark outside the house, having agreed on what they
would do if the mob came.

Well, it did come, in several cars with their headlights
on. The men, lying in ambush with nothing but shotguns
loaded with birdshot, waited until members of the mob
got out of their cars and started for the house. Then the
battle was on.

I do not know the whole story of what happened that
night, but what I heard was that there were some people
who were never seen again after that night. Some of the
mob members were carried away by their friends. It
appears that finally Gray's protectors ran out of am-
munition. When the mob left to get reinforcements,
Gray's friends recognized that this was the time to
retreat. Then the sharecroppers rushed into the house to
talk Gray into letting them take him to some place where
he might be safe. He refused, and his friends felt there
was nothing more they could do. They advised the women
to look after their personal safety.

Some of the men and boys went into the woods; some
went to their homes. The mob came back that night and
finished Ralph Gray. And the next day the Black manhunt was on. Almost all the Negro men and teenage boys
in that community who couldn't be cleared by their
landlords were jailed. Every day I would read the Birmingham papers to see what was going to happen to our
people around Camp Hill. And every day these papers
had news of protests from all over the world going into
the sheriff's office in Camp Hill and to the governor in
Montgomery. Some came from as far as Germany, Russia
and China.

They jailed about 30 men and boys, but finally they all
walked out free, without a trial, thanks to the strength of

the protest that had been built up. Of course, it was too late in the season for some of them to raise crops that year.

I have talked with some of these farmers, and I found they still had the highest respect for the ILD and the Communist Party for leading the struggle in 1931 in their behalf in Camp Hill, Alabama.

5

THE MAKING OF A UNION MAN AND A COMMUNIST

In spite of the constant battle to make a living, and such racist persecution as I have described, I still remained to some degree a happy-go-lucky sort of guy. I sang in quartets around Birmingham, having the reputation of being one of the best bass singers in that area. I had been singing for seven years and I got used to people following the quartet every Sunday from one church to another to hear my group sing.

So I wasn't at all surprised one day when a man I knew by sight, a Negro worker, named Al Murphy, greeted me warmly. This was around July 1931.

I said, "Where've you been? Ain't seen you 'round in a long time. Still in the shop?"

"I got fired."

"What for?"

He told me he'd been taking part in the campaign for the Scottsboro boys. The company had found out about it and fired him. He said he just got back from a conference in New York where the Scottsboro Case had been discussed.

I asked, "What are they saying about us up there?"

Well, he told me, they wondered why we didn't organize. He had told the conference that Southern Negroes felt they didn't have anvthing to fight with. They asked him whether it was easier to organize or to fight and he admitted that it was easier to organize.

I met him again in September and he asked me to come to a meeting that week at the home of a fellow named Lee, who worked in the same shop, saying that at this meeting we would organize for action. I thought for a minute of my grandmother saying the Yankees were coming back to finish the job of freeing the Negroes in the South. Every time there was an attack on my people I wondered when that day would come. When the Scottsboro Case was exposed as a frameup, when telegrams began to pour in from New York and other Northern states, as well as cables from all over Europe, I thought this was the time somebody was coming to help us do something to free ourselves. So when I heard the word "organize" I wanted to join up.

When I got to Lee's house, I expected to see a crowded room but was shocked to see only those I had been seeing every day in the shop or around in the community. There were about eight altogether. What kind of a meeting was this? Al Murphy began to talk about the Scottsboro Case, especially what it meant to the freedom struggle of the Black people. He discussed the jury system in the South, linking it to the fact that those boys had been given a death sentence by an all-white jury.

He said we had to stop the "legal lynching" of the eight who had been sentenced to death (one of them, a 12-year-old had been sent to the penitentiary till he was old enough to be tried). Murphy explained that the Scottsboro Case was only a part of the over-all oppression of our people.

"It's the system itself that brings about these frameups and lynchings," and went on to say he wanted all of us to understand that the kind of society in which we lived robbed the masses of people of a livelihood; that the only way the bosses could prevent the white and the Black masses of people from struggling together was to keep them divided. If they could spread the lie that every white woman was in danger of being raped by some Black man, it helped to spread fear and disunity. He gave us a little pamphlet with a map showing the whole area of the Black Belt. From the beginning, he said, the development of this area was carried on by the slave-holders who raised cotton for the most part. The Black population outnumbered the white. The Blacks built not only the railroads and the factories, they had helped to build the material wealth of the entire South with their toil and sweat and blood.

Yet we Negroes enjoyed practically none of the rights guaranteed American citizens by the U.S. Constitution.

I said to myself, "This man is a Communist!" I was at a Communist meeting and, though nothing sensational was happening, the idea was exciting.

He went on to explain what he meant by "Black Belt." Blacks constituted a majority of the population in many areas of the South. He pointed out that in these areas people like us were kept from voting, from running for public office and from taking part in self-government.

I said to myself, "Yes, when my grandmother, my mother, my brother and I and so many more of us hoped to go to school—and we never stopped hoping—we never did get a chance. Right here and now we Blacks are the last to be hired and the first to be fired. It was we, already existing on the crumbling edge of starvation, who suffered the highest death rate. If we had any medical care at all, it was just a whisper above being nothing!

When he said that not everybody could be a member of the Party, I wondered if I could be—or who among that gathering of eight Black men from the shop could be. To be members, the man said, people had to be willing to sacrifice a part of their good times; they had to give the time they saved to activity and education among other workers who felt something was wrong with the setup but didn't know what to do about it.

I sat there wondering if I could fit in; then I looked at the other fellows and realized not one of them could read or write. I myself had to spell out every word before I knew what it was.

Al Murphy went on to say Communists spread the Party's message by distributing its leaflets and its newspaper. He said they would hold regular meetings, get to them on time and pay dues regularly. Then he added the Party would expel members who got drunk or were loose in their moral conduct or careless in handling finances.

After he had made all these points—very calm, quiet and convincing—he stopped. There wasn't much that anybody could fail to understand and there weren't many questions. We all eight signed up, each paying 50 cents initiation fee and pledging 10 cents monthly dues, or more, based on our rate of pay. They elected me unit organizer.

In our brief meeting that night we agreed our main task would be among the workers in our shop. We'd pick out individual workers to make friends with and, in this way, we would be able, we hoped, to build the organization in the Stockham plant.

To come back to the shop, I mentioned in a previous chapter that I had told the foreman that the pay for the hard job we were doing ought not to be cut, and he said, "I'll let you know." (This was after the work had been put on the conveyor.) Well, when the speed-up reached its peak in 1931, they brought in a time-checker or worker-watcher to make reports on which our wage rates would be based. We were working on the machines now, where each man was capable of turning out triple or more the amount of work he used to do by hand. But were his wages tripled or even doubled? I don't have to tell you the answer.

As I've said, all of us molders were Black, and because of this we were not recognized as molders by the Stockham Pipe and Fittings Company. It classed us as "machine-runners." In the late 1920's at Stockham's, when they'd be having photos taken of the machines, the big supers would order us, the Black molders, to get back from our molding machines. Then the little straw bosses would stand beside the machines as if they were running them.

As for the time-checkers, these men with the watches in their hands and their eyes jumping from the watches to the workers and then back to the watches, for two days they kept track of how long it took us to do everything up to the second—from going to the toilet or getting a drink of hydrant water to getting back to our machines. On the basis of this two-day check the time-checker figured a rate for so many molds an hour. If he said 25 an hour, that's how many we had to produce—good ones—in order to stay out of the red.

We had to be at the machine at 6:30 a.m., even though our time didn't start until seven o'clock. We had to work until three p.m., after which we had to clean our machines; and it would be nearly half-past three by the time we could leave. The 30 minutes we were supposed to have for lunch gave us time to gulp our food as best we could, sometimes as we were hurrying back to the machines.

We worked under these conditions, with the foremen cussing and raw-hiding the men, until one cold day along about November.

We held our weekly unit meeting and reported on the conditions in the shop. A Party representative visited each meeting. This time he got us started on a series of actions. "For the next meeting," he said, "sit down and write your complaints just like you are writing a letter—the best you can."

At the next meeting we had our letter telling what the foreman had said to us; how he cussed out John; how one man was doing two men's work and not getting paid for it, and so on. We turned it over to the Party representative and he took it with him.

About two weeks later he brought it back—printed in the *Southern Worker*, weekly newspaper of the Communist Party, published in Chattanooga, Tennessee, with big headlines about conditions at the Stockham Pipe and Fittings Company plant. Our pride and excitement increased when we found out the letter also appeared in the *Sunday Worker*, published in New York. We read the papers as well as we could; we had never before been able to express our anger against these conditions like this, and we were hopeful that the people in the communities would get so indignant that Stockham's would be compelled to do something about them. The Party representative gave us all extra copies to distribute among the people, and one to put where the company stoolpigeon would get to it—actually we dropped it in his yard.

Another few days passed. Then one day the supers, worried-looking, came into the shop and said they didn't want anybody to leave for the bathhouse.

"We are going to have a meeting this evening. Nobody changes until after the meeting."

It was on the right-hand side of the shop, out in the open, in a broad space near a brick wall and the fence. Everybody was out there—Black molders and white machinists, the assistant super, the super himself and other supervisory personnel, including Mr. Nibley, the personnel director, who got up and said that he wanted to tell the men that, "beginning tomorrow, we don't want a man to put his hand on a machine before seven or he's fired. You-all will stop work at 2:45 and clean up your machine by three and be ready to go to the bathhouse."

He went over that again and again. "Times are getting hard," he said, "and we'll have to be cutting wages but I want to tell you men right now we don't want anybody to work more time than you-all supposed to. Stop for lunch when the whistle blows, at 12. Be ready to start work when the 12:30 whistle blows. Stop work at 2:45, clean up your machines, and be ready to get out of here by three o'clock."

I almost burst out laughing when he said, "If any foreman cusses at any man here, he won't have any more job here . . . and the same goes for you fellows." What made it funny, in a crazy sort of way, was his lumping "you fellows"—meaning John Bedell, me, any number of other Black workers in the shop—in the same bag with the superintendents, assistant supers and straw bosses. Suppose one of those white guys did get fired for cussing us—and chances stood a thousand to one against it—he'd have another job before sundown. But let one of us get fired for "standing up" to or "talking back" to a white "bossman" and we might as well decide right then and there to get clean out of the state, because we'd be blackballed at every factory gate for hundreds of miles around.

Anyhow, when the meeting was over, the men all went out full of joy, and some of us said, "Them papers sure did stir things up!" and things like, "If they tell us to strike, I'm ready."

Black workers and white workers—all were openly talking about "this great victory," talking to anyone or everyone who would listen. And among the first talkers were the Communists. The Party put out leaflets calling on workers to organize, Blacks and whites together, for higher wages, job security, unemployment and social insurance for all unemployed. But the inexperienced Party leadership in the South didn't yet know how to guard itself or warn us in the shop unit to watch out for the traps our enemy set.

6
BOSSES AND STOOL-PIGEONS

Our information about the company's stoolpigeons came from a non-Party friend, the wife of a foundry worker who had acted as a stoolie. In the plant, a trusted Stockham official had the job of supervising the flock of stoolpigeons, both white and Black. Their main job would be to find out who was behind the "plot" to distribute leaflets on plant property. The setup consisted of a bunch of spies, our own fellow-workers and shopmates, who were paid $5 each every week, based on the report they pushed through the pay-window in a sealed envelope. If they didn't have anything to report, they would write, "no news," but get paid just the same. The envelopes were all opened by the "trusted official."

One of the eight of us who had joined the Party that night, I found out later, was the first guy to sign up with the boss to pigeon on us. When our second meeting ended, as we later recalled, the unit members had asked where we would meet next time and the question was left hanging. The spy came to me soon after and said he'd be glad if we held the meeting at his house.

That would have made everything easy for him; after we had cleared out, he could write his report while everything was still fresh in his mind—all our names, who said what, who objected. He would then be ready to stick the report in the pay-window.

Nevertheless, even at the Stockham plant, with all its wealth and ability to buy spies, we ordinary Black workers didn't come off too badly. Our unit structure, in spite of lack of experience, helped us to function as long as we did, and as long as we functioned we became a training school for men who later helped to make great labor history in Alabama.

In the course of time we set up throughout the Stockham Pipe and Fittings plant six Communist Party groups, each unknown to the others (except for the leaders of the units). The reason, obviously, was to protect members from stoolpigeons. I was organizer of Unit 1, which was reponsible for Units Number 2, 3, 4, 5 and 6.

Our policy paid off well. The guy that stooled on us in Unit 1 caused some damage when he handed in all our names, but the damage was confined to one unit. He knew nothing about the other five. Though he did his dirty little job and got his five bucks reward, he did not know that a non-Party intimate of his had exposed him to us before the next meeting. When he asked where it was being held, nobody seemed to have found out.

When my friend John Bedell was fired, we workers were upset. What could we do to stop the firings? The shops were operating only two or three days a week during this blustery-cold January of 1932, with snow flurries whipping across Birmingham. Negro molders on the conveyors were earning 30 cents an hour base pay.

It was during this period that I attended a get-together of unit organizers on the South Side at which the C.P. industrial organizer for the South, Harry Jackson, was present. He advised us to try to get the names of some white workers in the shop. He talked about the necessity, the day-to-day importance, of political activity among white workers, saying that this was the correct Marxist-Leninist approach. I just couldn't see myself or any other Black man carrying this out, although I agreed with him in principle. Jackson insisted that everybody in the shop ought to try to find white contacts and then the white comrades would visit their houses.

Not long after that the shop had its annual Community Chest meeting, sponsored by the company, where they asked every worker for a day's pay. A white man from the galvanizing department was good and mad about giving to the Community Chest when we were not making anything ourselves. "We need someone to help us," he said. I didn't say anything to him then. A few days after that I saw him again and decided to speak to him. At this time I was working just one or two days a week.

"I met a white guy on the street," I said, "who told me he wanted to talk to some white fellows in the shop."

That was all I had time to say at that moment. Not long after I met Harry Jackson, and he warned me that this white guy was one of the Stockham stoolies. In the meantime, the weekly *Southern Worker* and *Sunday Worker* had been brought to the shop by the man who was the literature agent of our unit. These papers attracted the stoolpigeons like breadcrumbs attract pigeons in the park. We distributed them every Friday.

When I walked out of the shop that Friday evening, the same white man came up to me, saying, "You seen that white man any more about coming to my house?"

"White man?" I said. "What white man?"

He said, "You're the man who said you had somebody who wanted to talk to me."

I told him he must be mistaken; he must mean somebody else; I'd never said I had a white man who wanted to talk to him. He insisted he thought I was the one, and I told him there was somebody in the shop who looked so much like me that some people took us for brothers. He gave me a sort of doubting look and walked away.

When I went back to work the following Tuesday morning, the personnel manager, Nibley, asked me how long I had been with the company. I said seven years. Then he asked if I lived in one of the company houses and I told him that I did. Had I paid rent when my leg was broken in a motorcycle accident? I said, "No, sir."

"Well, I want that house," Nibley said.

"What's the trouble?" I asked him.

"Nothing. I just want that house."

"I ain't had no trouble with the foreman," I told him, "nor with the company, nor with the community, and I been with the company seven years. So it seems funny that I got to get out now and no reason given."

"I want to put someone I know in that house."

"Seems to me," I said, "I been here long enough for you to know me."

"Yes, I know you, all right, but I don't know *of* you."

I had ten days to get out of the house. I didn't have anywhere to move to, and I told Nibley that even if I found a place I wouldn't have any money to pay for it.

He asked if I could find a house and how much I thought I'd need. I said I thought I could get a house for $10. He loaned me the money. We moved Saturday; one of the fellows from the unit helped me.

I went to work again the following Monday. I was getting ready to go to the bathhouse and clean myself up that evening when word came for me not to leave; Mr. Darvin wanted to see me. So I stayed after everybody else had left the shop and it was getting to feel like the inside of an icebox. Finally the assistant super Darvin came and took me out to the far side of the building. I wondered why, when the weather was so bitter. In this open space in the darkening twilight, he started to talk.

"Hudson, what's that I hear you're in?"

"What you mean, Mr. Darvin?"

"You're in something."

I said, "I got to know what you talking about. I'm a member of my church; I sing bass in the glee club; I'm in my church club, the Gleaners' band, the Home Department of the Sunday school." I thought a second or two and I added, "Oh, yes, I'm in the Junior Deacon's Board . . . I can't think of nothing else I'm in."

Like a man that's had both ears jammed all the time we were talking, Darvin acted like he hadn't heard a word, and he said, "Well, if you tell me what you're in, maybe I can help you."

I said, "What d'you mean 'help' me? You mean I'm fired?"

"Yes," he said, "You're fired."

I asked if he had my time made out. He did. I asked if he had my statement with him. He had.

"You might as well give it to me, Mr. Darvin," I said, "because somebody's lying about me, and if I don't have a chance to defend myself, what can I do but go?"

When I went to wash up after I left him, I found out why he had wanted to get so far away from the shop even though we would have been alone inside. The fact was that many of the guys in my shop had stayed to watch what was happening, and Darvin didn't intend for them to hear. Some of the fellows, of course, wondered whose turn was next.

When I went back to the Stockham paymaster the following Tuesday to get my $18 paycheck, I found they had deducted the $10 advanced to me for the house.

A few days later I was told to get in touch with a Party section organizer from New York, a white comrade named Burns, and after he had heard the long chronicle of happenings in the shop, he said we should call a meeting of Unit 1 for Saturday morning, and he would come. We notified tbe leaders of the other five units, so when he arrived our whole leadership met him. We were able to give him all the facts—the names of the stool-pigeons, what jobs they worked on, where they lived, and so on. He made a note of all this information.

Then we planned that the leaflet Burns would write and get back to us would be distributed by us in our community that night. We waited until dark and because of the bitter cold we were not worried about running into any of our neighbors or acquaintances.

Those hundreds of leaflets we clutched in our frostbit-ten fingers explained the company's stoolpigeon setup. We put them on everybody's porch in our community that night, especially on the porches of the six stoolpigeons. The name of each of them was mentioned, what depart-ment he worked in, the kind of job he worked on, and his home address. Yes, we put them in all the yards, on the church steps and under the church doors. It was one of the most satisfying leaflet distributions I have ever had anything to do with.

The leaflet, as it developed, was rather effective in another way. We heard later that a couple of the spies, with fistfuls of leaflets, walked clear across Birmingham and climbed the mountain on the outskirts to the man-sion where the biggest boss, Mr. Stockham, lived. That meant bringing the two battle lines closer together. What was going to happen next?

Now, from the time I left the farm to work on the railroad in Atlanta in 1923, and in all my months and years of toil there and at the Stockham plant, where I went in the winter of 1924 in hopes of earning the big wage of $5 a day, my one desire was to look out for the welfare of Lucy, my wife, and our little boy, Hosea, no matter what happened.

I had to see to it that my family would have a house to live in, food in the kitchen. And when the paymaster that freezing January afternoon in 1932 handed me my last paycheck of $8, the outlook for our future was like that on a cold, moonless night. Nothing like this had happened since we got married. How was I going to tell Lucy?

I decided to tell her straight out. She didn't speak for a while and she seemed quite calm. Then she said, "We'll make out somehow. You've only been working one and two days a week, anyhow." This was true for the whole shop at that time. Then she said, "It'd be better if you could get on the city welfare. Then at least you wouldn't have to work so hard for such little money."

The idea of going on welfare gave me a big headache. Anyway, how could I ever get on welfare without the recommendation of the Stockham foundry bosses?

I couldn't sleep that cold night for trying to figure out how I could go and apply for relief. Finally, I got an idea and I dozed off into sleep.

I happened to know of an old white man in Birmingham named Saul, whose job, I was told, was to go around to Negroes and solicit petty cases for groups of lawyers. I got out early that Wednesday morning and walked toward his office—I wanted to catch this man before he took the elevator up into the building.

I met him in the lobby and told him I'd been fired from the Stockham foundry and that the boss wouldn't tell me why he was firing me.

He said: "Wasn't some trouble out there about some papers that's being distributed in the shops? Do you know anything about that?"

I said that I didn't. He then asked me how much money I had. I told him all I had left was $2.

"I'm going to give you a letter to the Welfare. You tell them you've been working for me but I don't have anything else for you to do."

He wrote the letter and handed it to me and took my last two dollars.

At the Welfare office I gave it to a Mrs. Brooks and told her what he said. After sitting and waiting until afternoon for her to answer I was put on relief. She gave me a $2 ticket—something like the food stamps you see nowadays—with which I was supposed to buy a week's food for me and my family. I picked up the tickets regularly each week after that. But we didn't have any meat for months later.

My friend Bedell was still looking for work. We'd stand on the street corner there in East Birmingham, shivering in the cold and trying to keep each other's spirits up, just talking.

One night I said, "You know what? I reckon I'll go back to Atlanta." At the time I didn't know what I would do in Atlanta because I sure didn't have any connections there. But after I'd said it, the idea seemed pretty good, and I said, "Yes, that's just what I'm going to do." We both knew it was useless to keep on looking for a job around Birmingham.

"You know, Hudson," Bedell said, after a while. "You're the only one I got to depend on. I come up here from Columbus (Georgia), and I've been here a long time. I can't go back there." He went on, "Don't anybody down there know me any more; all my folks is dead. Everybody I know's right around here in Birmingham."

Then he straight out asked me not to go; and I must say I felt better when I agreed not to; it seemed like we were blood brothers.

Bedell and I walked in the cold night and we stood on the little footbridge over the drainage ditch. I said we'd get together. "You find somebody and I'll find somebody, and we'll rebuild our unit."

What had happened after we got fired was that all the rest of our Party unit got scared and quit. At the same time though, we remembered how we had built the Party in the shop to about 35 members in a few groups. When they fired me, all of them began to draw away like mice when the cat was around. Anyway, soon afterward, everybody else was laid off. Bedell and I tried to figure out who to see.

Joe Howard, a friend of Bedell's, was working in the galvanizing pit; Bedell said he'd go to work on Joe. I told him I'd work on Obi Mayfield, an old friend of mine and on relief, who was working at a welfare job in the East Lake Park along with me. When I began to talk with him about the Party, he said, "You in that? I been seeing these papers around but I didn't know who was putting 'em out." He finally said he'd be glad to join. Then we got another fellow, Wes, and still another, John.

We regrouped our unit and decided on a regular meeting date. We began to read again and understand more about the Party and the history of the working class. We cut out Sunday school attendance so we could save the time for the unit meetings; after Sunday morning classes, we all went to church.

It began to look as if everybody was unemployed. And that meant everybody was hungry part of the time or without fuel to heat their houses during that cold winter, or unable to pay a doctor or, for that matter, even to pay for their family funerals. Many a real estate company was glad for somebody to stay in a house, even without rent, because if they put a family out, the unemployed workers would wreck the house and take it away for fuel by night. Even in daylight, some stood on the street blocks away watching for the police patrol while their neighbors or friends got wood from a wrecked building. This was a kind of free-for-all, a share-the-wealth situation.

Men, women and children got involved together many times. When the railroad coal cars were nearby, young men and boys would go up to the tracks at night with bags, climb up on the train and roll off the coal. Next morning early, grown folks with sacks and children with baskets would hurry to the railroad to pick up the coal. Sometimes even the firemen, who was generally Black, would shovel off coal from the tender of the locomotive as if he were throwing it into his firebox.

For clothing, most workers just patched and patched. Doctors? You could just forget them. Funerals? There were plenty of them in all the poor sections of Birmingham and burials were in the cheapest pine caskets.

In April 1933, after I'd been on relief for more than a year, we moved from the East Birmingham community to North Birmingham, or Collegeville, which put me under a new set of welfare officials. When I applied for a grocery order, there was a long delay—which meant no food—although I walked downtown day after day. Finally, one morning, a visitor, Mannin, who was white, came to my house while I was still haunting the welfare office, left a blank form on which I had to fill out the place where I worked last.

Oh, oh, I thought, but I went and looked for the old white man who had signed for me before and I couldn't find him anywhere. He had left the office building and nobody could tell me where he might be. So here I was, right back where I had been the year before when I was trying to get on welfare without having to refer to the Stockham bosses.

I kept that blank for more than a week, and I continued to go down to the welfare office. I registered for food, without any result. And one day I took that blank form to the Stockham employment window.

Nibley walked to the window and said, "What do you want?" I pushed the envelope toward him and asked: "Will you fill this blank for me?" Finally he got his pen and began to write. When he finished he went and got a large envelope and put the form into it, sealed it, and handed the envelope back. I went home and got me a steam pot and opened that envelope and read his answers.

One of the questions went something like this: "When your works open up again will this party be eligible for his job?" Nibley had answered that one, "No." Next question: "If not, will you state why?" His answer was, "This man is against our form of government."

I put the sheet back in the envelope, resealed it and sent it on to the welfare office. Mannin sent for me. I asked for him as he had instructed me to do in his notes to me.

His first words were, "I don't know whether you're going to like what I have to say. And I don't care if you don't like it. Why didn't you tell us when you first got on welfare that you was fired from your job because you was a Red?"

"Is that what they told you?" I asked. Mannin said, "Yes."

"They didn't tell me that, " I said. "All they told me was that they wanted the house I was living in, and when I asked them what was the trouble, they said they wanted somebody they knew to have the house."

"I don't know what was told to you," he said, but he didn't seem quite so rigid any more. He said, "I'm going to give you a grocery order and I'll mail your work slip, but don't you go out there on the job creating strikes and strife."

I told him I spent half my time taking care of my

business and the other half leaving the other man's business alone. After that run-in with Mannin, my work card and grocery slip always came on time.

7

UNEMPLOYMENT STRUGGLES

My first welfare job was out at East Lake Park, where they were tearing down the old swings and slides and seesaws and putting in new ones. They even put in a new swimming pool—none of this, naturally, for us Black folks who were doing the work.

That was a welfare job to be remembered. At first we found pennies in the sand and in the bottom of the old swimming pool. The whole thing for a while was like a kind of game—we were always hoping for a bigger find. Then one day a fellow cleaning out an old boat pulled a mess of mud and junk from under the seat. We were working by ourselves—no supervision—when this fellow pulls out a billfold all covered with muck from under that seat.

Now that man was working hard, like all the rest of us, and the pay he got came from the supply house—so many pounds a day of beans, so many cans of tomatoes, so much rice, prunes, potatoes. But, as I've said, no meat, no coffee or sugar—and, of course, no money, even for rent. The billfold had $90 in it and that was a lot of money for that worker. No one begrudged it to him.

We worked there about a year and then they opened a gardening project. They put hundreds of people out across the fields—just vacant land—digging up the ground for planting. There were not only digging crews; there were also raking and planting crews. At the same time, Welfare had another big project under way on the road that crawled up and over the Red Mountain and the Shades Mountain, linking Birmingham and Montgomery.

This narrow mountain highway had been the cause of many deaths; a car's brakes would give out on one of these steep, narrow, curving passages, and it was goodbye. So this was important enough in itself to rate top-priority engineering, but here was the Welfare Department using these unskilled, unemployed Black men to dig up and move heavy rocks and grade the road, and to do other work that machines ought to do. And maybe we wouldn't be grouching about it so much, hard as it was, but the pay we were getting was that same mess of groceries.

Well, a group of four of us decided we would have to do something, though we didn't know just what, because how did you tackle the Welfare Department? We finally began walking up and down the various welfare projects, inviting the workers, Black and white, to come to a mass meeting on Friday afternoon. It was to be held at the Kingston School in East Birmingham. At least 400 men and women attended.

We told them how we put in all that backbreaking labor, digging out rocks as if we were doing an important highway construction job, as if we were getting two, three, four or five dollars an hour instead of two, three, four or five grocery slips—depending on how many were in the family. We said we ought to demand cash money for this work, and this led, naturally, to a discussion about going to see the city commissioner, Jimmie Jones, in Birmingham. It was moved and voted, that Friday afternoon, to march to City Hall Saturday morning.

About 150 showed up for the 2-1/2-mile march to

Birmingham. We formed a line four-deep and walked down, on the way electing a committee of six spokesmen—five men and one woman. Only one white had come. One of the spokesmen was a 19-year-old Black worker.

At City Hall the delegation stepped back against the curb, facing the building where the city government was located, and then we started to go up to see City Commissioner Jones. Detectives Mosely and Elliott (Mosely, the chief city detective, was said to have killed two or three people) stood facing us, guarding the City Hall entrance.

"Where you niggers going?" Mosely asked.

"We're going to Commissioner Jones' office."

He asked the lone white man, "You with this gang? You going to Jimmie Jones' office, too?"

"No," the white man said, "I'm going to the Health Department."

So he deserted us right there, leaving five Blacks. Mosely pulled out his pistol and drove us back down the steps. We stood in front of City Hall on the sidewalk.

"Fellow workers!" the 19-year-old called out. "These gentlemen won't let us see Mr. Jones now, so we're going back, but we're going to reinforce our strength, and we're coming back and we *are* going to see Mr. Jones."

I had never heard or seen anything like that. As for Mosely, I guess he never had either; he rushed in and punched the boy on the side of the head, yelling, "I thought I told you niggers to get out from here!"

Two or three of the guys began to ball their fists up and stepped toward Mosely. The other detective, Elliott, was just standing there watching.

Gradually everything calmed down before any real violence started, and we marched up the street to Second Avenue and back up to the Kingston School where we had started from. When we got there we had about 50 marchers left.

We heard later that Jimmie Jones and other city officials had got so scared that you'd have thought we were coming back that same day. Policemen on the roofs of buildings around City Hall and across the street had machine guns pointed down at the sidewalks, waiting for us. They stayed there from the time we left, around 11 o'clock, till late that afternoon. By that time, of course, we had all gone home or about our business. Later we heard that City Commissioner Jones had a special group of police take him home in an ambulance. Maybe he figured on having help in getting rushed to the hospital if anything happened to him.

Well, we didn't go back that day. But on November 7th the same year a mass meeting was called on the Jefferson County Court House steps, with all unemployed workers invited, to raise the question of more relief. There were, according to newspaper accounts, more than 7,000 people present—the greatest such meeting in the history of Birmingham. Men and women, Black and white, some with baskets, some with little carts. They didn't understand; they thought they were going to get food.

A committee of nine, led by a Birmingham-raised young white woman, Mary Leonard, went down to see Jimmie Jones. And on that committee, there was one Black man, James Cooper.

In the commissioner's office, with all the police and detectives standing around, what was discussed was pay for our labor on these so-called jobs and more relief for the people who didn't have any jobs.

Jimmie Jones didn't want to hear about more relief. He began to holler, interrupting the members of the committee. Finally, he asked Mary Leonard, "Do you believe in social equality for niggers?" She said, "Yes, why not? Negroes are just as good as you or me, so why not have social equality?"

He said, "I've got no more to say to you! No more to do with you!"

He said to the officers, "I want you-all to go to the Court House and get all that gang away from there."

At the Court House the police rushed up to the top of the steps, and one of them yelled, "Listen, you-all! There ain't no use you're standing there." A few minutes later a group of 10 to 15 deputies attacked the largely white crowd. It was the first time for most of them to be treated like Negroes had been treated all along in the South.

A campaign of postcard protests had in the meanwhile been organized by the committee and they had been pouring into Jimmie Jones' office.

The result was that a few concessions were made to the unemployed, and that was about all, until the Roosevelt government in 1933 came in with the Civil Works Administration. But even before that, even there in the Birmingham struggles, there were still other results from that Negro-white demonstration at the city commissioner's office and other similar demonstrations. Such struggles raised the level of Negro-white unity and proved that Black and white could unite like brothers and sisters to fight the class enemy as they would unite and fight a pack of wild animals, no matter what hard feelings might have existed between them.

We didn't have any organized Party leadership at this particular period, but we still had meetings with representatives "coming through."

A committee of Unit Organizers was set up in 1932 to reorganize the Party, which had been first established in the Birmingham area in 1930. It was later known as the Section Bureau which consisted of leaders of the local party, people in and around Birmingham, and they were all people who had key responsibilities.

One member, for example, was responsible for the unemployed; a second for literature; a third for work among the coal miners; another for activity among the steel-workers; a fifth was responsible for working among and organizing the women. All of them, along with the representatives of a higher committee (as well as the ILD committee working on the Scottsboro Case) constituted the Communist Party setup when it finally got reorganized for action in the Birmingham area

Each one of these people in the key positions was also a leader in a unit, in the section and a leader at the place where any one of the Party units happened to be meeting. For instance, if a person was responsible for two or three Party units in an area, the unit organizers would meet this person, who would collect both reports and dues at the same time—reports covering the unit's activities, the unemployed situation, what was happening in steel, etc.—because each unit was responsible for concentrating on and making contact with steelworkers and coal miners, as well as keeping posted on all questions affecting the unemployed locally and nationally.

In other words, we had a network of leadership—and it was not a conspiratorial leadership; rather, it was organized in such a way that in a few hours everybody in and around Birmingham could be contacted and informed. In the units, we had subcaptains—out of the members of each unit of nine, the organizer had the help of two who looked after the other seven. If a member were sick or didn't show up at a meeting, we wouldn't wait until the next get-together to find out what had happened. The subcaptain would make contact right away and find out the cause.

In this way we were able to keep the whole membership alert on the Scottsboro Case or on whatever came up to affect the workers' interests. We were able to move

people into action quickly. This is what we did, for
instance, when the Reeltown Sheriffs attacked the sharecroppers and the tenant farmers in 1932.

8

VICTORIES AND SETBACKS

In January, 1933, around Reeltown, there was a fairly
well-to-do Negro farmer, Clifford James, who owned his
livestock—hogs, cows, mules and so on. Nevertheless he
owed $6 to a white merchant in Reeltown; most farmers,
Black and white, had to buy on credit once in a while.

When Clifford James received his parity check from
the U.S. Government—the payment that certain farmers
got for limiting or not planting specified crops—he didn't
pay the merchant right away and the small debt rocked
on into the fall. At this point the merchant sent a deputy
sheriff to make a levy on Clifford James's livestock.
James said he would pay his bill when he sold his cotton
but he wouldn't let them take his livestock. The deputy
sheriff cussed him out and said, as he was leaving, that
he would be back to take his property anyway.

He came back with reinforcements. And it was whites
against Blacks, because by now James had notified
members of the Sharecroppers Union. When the deputies
came, the Black men had already elected a committee of
three to meet the white men and discuss the matter.
Clifford James was himself in the group; the other two
were Judd Moss and Mylo Bentley.

James and Bentley had got out into the yard and were
approaching the deputy sheriffs but Moss didn't get any
farther than the door. The sheriffs opened fire and shot
Moss dead as he was walking out of the door. It was

reported that they hit Bentley, but they didn't wound Clifford James.

Much later than the time when these events occurred I visited Reeltown and heard the story from people who had witnessed the murder. They said it was snowing while the deputies and the sharecroppers were shooting at each other and that the battle was joined in by Black men who had been hunting. Some of the deputy sheriffs were wounded by gunshot.

The Black men left and scattered out through the woods. Just before dark that evening it seems that Clifford James went back to see what had been done there. He was wounded, but at least alive. He found sides of his bacon thrown all over the floor, barrels of syrup poured on top of the bacon and flowing inches deep and covering the floor.

He and Bentley made it to the Tuskegee Institute. Surely two Black men would be safe there, if they could be safe anywhere in the South: Clifford James, it was said, knew a Negro doctor there who would treat him and Bentley. The doctor took James and Mylo into his office, and, according to press reports, notified the high sheriff that he had captured these "dangerous criminals." In Kilby prison, without being given any treatment for their wounds, forced to sleep on the cold floor, both men, according to officials' statements, died from exposure, but they can be said to have been murdered.

The ILD got in touch with the widows of the men and they gave the organization permission to attend to the burial. A committee arranged for a Montgomery undertaker to prepare the bodies and ship them to Birmingham. The Welsh Brothers, in North Birmingham, had agreed to do it, but when the bodies arrived, they did not go to get them. When the ILD local people went to the Welsh Brothers, they were told the city officials had forbidden the bodies to be moved.

The committee finally went to Hickman Jordan, a Negro undertaker with a very poorly equipped place and one hearse pulled by horses. He told them that he would look after burying the dead, while they took care of looking after the living.

"I own my place from Hell to Heaven," he said. "I pay for my license to bury the dead. I'll go get the bodies and keep them here as long as you want till you get ready to take them to the cemetery."

At the committee's request they were placed in a room where anyone could come and view these men, whom they considered to have been lynched by landlords in south Alabama.

Some 20,000 handbills were put out around Birmingham and its suburbs—Fairfield, Bessemer and Ensley, calling on all who wanted to view the dead men and announcing the funeral for the following Friday.

Meanwhile, city officials complained to Jordan that these bodies were stirring up "too much animosity," and he'd have to hurry and bury them, but Jordan just asked them, "What law is being violated?"

"It ain't a question of violating the law," they answered. "It's just a question of too much animosity being stirred up around those two dead niggers."

"If you want these bodies buried now," Jordan said, "You'll have to bury them yourself. My customers wanted them buried on Friday. The funeral is going to be at 11 o'clock, and they're paying me to do what they tell me to."

"If you ain't going to bury them," they said, "we want you to close them up. We don't want people stopping and looking at them."

The result was that the caskets stayed open, where the people, white and Black, could view the bodies.

On Friday the police were seen everywhere in the

Black community, especially in the North Birmingham area around Collegeville and Vulcan City. They had told Blacks in the area, "There's not going to be any funeral. Get out of the yard!"

Along about 10 o'clock that morning, when the crowds began walking down the railroad from all directions—nobody had money to ride—there were as many as six or seven thousand, and practically every policeman in town, too, including the chief, was there. What could they do now? They sat in their cars watching, and they warned Jordan, "Just don't let them block the traffic."

There were so many people that they covered the vacant area of about a block in front of the undertaker's place. They couldn't get a minister to preside though there were several of them in that great mass of people. Finally, a man named Crystal—a World War I veteran and a local ILD organizer—made the funeral oration.

Six or seven white women came in to the hall and sat in the midst of the Black audience. When the police saw these women, they went to Jordan again and told him he would have to get them out.

Jordan told them, "If there are any white folks you want out, you'll have to go and get them out yourself, because I ain't goin' to bar no folks."

A policeman went in and talked to the white women who were seated in the middle row of a bench in the middle of the hall. "You-all are going to have to come out from there." One of them was Mary Leonard, who led the committee of the unemployed down at Jimmie Jones's office. All of them just looked back at him and stayed put. He was afraid to go in and get them because he would have had to drag them out. So he just had to leave them alone.

It was said that this was the biggest Negro funeral ever held in Birmingham, because in addition to the

mourners the city's whole police department, led by
motor cycles and police cars, made traffic just back up
and wait.

Back in the Louisiana parishes there was also a big
movement of sharecroppers and tenant farmers. Some
were able to win a few concessions from the landlord-
farmers. Many had to move to New Orleans, Baton
Rouge and other cities and towns because the local
federal farming agencies made it impossible for these
Black men to survive as farmers.

In Alabama particular credit must go to Joe Gelders
and the role he played in the 1930's. A professor who had
lost his job because of his position on civil rights, he
continued to fight, and he organized a Civil Rights
Committee. He played a strong part in bringing liberal
whites into the Scottsboro struggle.

In Gadsden, the mayor of the town, the sheriff, the big
coal and steel operators and other industrialists said they
wouldn't ever allow any union to be organized. When the
union organizers were being beat up and run out (many
union members were reported "missing"), it was Joe
Gelders and his committee who went into Gadsden and
held an open hearing that lasted several days. Some
members of the Roosevelt Administration gave their
support to the unionists.

As a result of that hearing, the CIO, under John L.
Lewis's leadership, was eventually able to make a break-
through in Gadsden, organizing the rubber workers, the
Republic Steel workers and many other workers in an
area that had been considered a little Hitler Germany.

At a hearing in Washington, D.C., Joe Gelders exposed
the eleven National Guard officers who were said to be on
the payroll of the Tennessee Coal and Iron Company for
the sole purpose of keeping union "agitators" from the
ranks of the workers and to prevent strikes by Negro coal

miners. The National Guard was used to break up the picket lines when the miners went out on strike.

Soon after Joe Gelders set up his civil rights committee, the enemy got to him. Some hoodlums beat him up in Birmingham and threw him into a gulley, leaving him for dead. He played it cool until he got out of the hospital, and then he complained to the LaFollette Senate Committee which was set up to investigate strike-breaking by the corporations. An investigation was made and it was proved that the National Guardsmen were on the payroll.

In Birmingham, the papers said, whether it was true or not, that an order came from the officials of U.S. Steel that they would have to cease such activities—terror against the workers, carrying National Guard officers on the company payroll, and so forth.

Joe Gelders had identified Dent Williams as one of the gang that beat him up and left him for dead in the gulley. He had got away with shooting Willie Peterson. Did he think he could get away with this, too? A news reporter went to Dent Williams in Birmingham and asked him if he had a statement to make and if he was going to Washington. He said he didn't have any business in Washington and the only way he would go would be if they'd come and get him.

But there had been a big upheaval and when it all cooled down Negroes were able to meet in social gatherings at their homes without being intimidated by the police, and the same was true in the union hall. It was Joe Gelders' fight that helped make this possible.

When the CIO came into the picture, Black steel workers in small miscellaneous shops joined because they felt this was what they were looking for. But it was difficult to convince the majority of the whites of the importance of coming into the union and struggling alongside the Black workers. Most of the whites said they wouldn't mind joining if they could have a union local to themselves—they didn't want to sit in the hall with the Negroes.

One of the worst offenders was the district representative of the steel workers. He would go about in meetings making insulting remarks to Negroes, always implying: "You boys feel you're as good as whites but that doesn't make you as good; and it doesn't mean you should have the same things, just because you feel you should."

At a meeting when we had the hall packed, he would say, "We can't get those whites, poor devils, to come out. But you-all stick here with us. We're going to see to it that you get better conditions, that you have more meat on your plates and that your kids don't leave the table hungry."

This went on from 1936 through 1938 and in the meantime we didn't have a check-off system. Although we had a contract with the Tennessee Coal and Iron Railroad Company, the newspapers were saying the TCI Steel Company would never recognize the CIO union and never sign a contract. But the workers did get a ten-cent raise in 1938, and we won the right to represent the members of the union when they had grievances.

In 1938, when I became unemployed again, like thousands of other workers I got a WPA job and joined the Workers Alliance. Three officers, including myself, went to Washington to see Harry Hopkins, head of the WPA and the Public Works Administration (PWA), as well as Aubrey Williams, who was youth administrator for Hopkins. We were seeking more projects and more relief.

In Washington we found that Alabama's Representative, Joe Sturins, from up around Gadsden, was on the floor of the House fighting against our having more projects, while Representative Luther Patrick, from Jefferson County, was fighting for them. We came back home, and I, along with Tom Howard and John Donovan, reported at a mass meeting behind the Jefferson County court house. Thousands came, Black and white, and the result was that the question of qualifying ourselves to vote was put at the top of our political agenda. We had to get people like Joe Sturins out of Washington and support people like Luther Patrick, who was fighting for the interests of the unemployed.

The whites went down to the Registration Board to register. So did I, with five other Negroes. When I filled out my blank, I was told I would be notified if I passed, but the whites filled out their blanks and were given certificates then and there. So the whites and I went to the offices of Attorney Arthur Shores and filed a petition for a court hearing. My white companions signed up as witnesses in my behalf. Judge McElroy said he wouldn't take any action against board members that day (it was Friday), but the following Monday all of us who had filed our petitions received our certificates in the mail and became qualified voters.

At about this time Roosevelt appointed a committee to investigate conditions in the South. On the basis of its findings, the President issued a statement declaring the South was the Nation's number one economic problem.

Liberals in the South were very much affected by that statement and seemed to want to do something about the situation. They called a Southwide conference early in the fall of 1938 in Birmingham, headed by such people as Eleanor Roosevelt, Mary McLeod Bethune, well-known Negro educator, and Supreme Court Justice Hugo Black. Delegates came from churches, Sunday schools, labor and professional organizations, and from the colleges.

The conference was organized into panels on different subjects: housing, women's rights, youth, civil rights, and so on. I was able to attend the conferences on housing and on women's rights in the Tutweiler Hotel, which Mrs. Roosevelt attended.

The Tutweiler didn't allow Negroes to enter through the lobby but on this occasion I went right through the front by way of the lobby and up to the conference room, without any trouble. Before that—and after—Negroes had to go up on the freight elevator at the rear of the building.

On the Sunday before the conference was to start, there was a big mass meeting in the city Municipal Auditorium, called by the Workers Alliance. Speakers talked to the packed house about conditions among the unemployed, white and Black, and about the importance of struggling for more jobs. I was one of the speakers.

On Monday, when the conference was called at the same place, everybody assembled and people sat wherever they could find seats. There were no complaints about the mingling of Black and white; everything was peaceful and quiet.

That night there was a mass meeting. Various leaders spoke, and again it was a mixed audience—no complaints, no criticism. On Tuesday morning, however, when the conference was scheduled to reconvene, Birmingham officials had roped the place off. From the street, straight across to the front of the auditorium, they had strung a white cord down through the main floor and up to the speakers' platform—one side for colored and the other for white.

Blacks had to go around to the side entrance, then enter on the side marked "Negroes"; whites went in on the side marked "White."

The period between 1937 and 1940 was one of rough-and-tumble struggles and new developments for workers in the South, especially in Alabama. In the spring of 1937 new forces joined in the fight of the Negro people and of labor for freedom. A Southern Negro Youth Conference was called to a convention in Richmond, Virginia, and young Black men and women—along with some young whites—set up the Southern Negro Youth Congress (SNYC). Headquarters was established in Richmond, Virginia, the home of James E. Jackson, one of the founders. Later, along with other young leaders, he helped to organize some 3,000 tobacco and other workers into the CIO in that city and state. Other fearless Black leaders who came out of that founding convention were Henry O. Mayfield, Edward E. Strong, Ethel Lee Goodman and Louis E. Burnham.

The second SNYC conference, held in the spring of 1938 in Chattanooga, was well attended by both Black and white youths, but this time there were also many adult delegates representing religious, social, fraternal and labor groups. Out of that strictly working conference, there came a clear and militant program on the problems confronting Negro youth.

In 1938, I was a delegate from Local 1489, United Steel Workers. It was Ed Strong, whom I thought of as a most courageous young man, who got me interested in joining. He himself was a wonderfully persuasive speaker.

The question was asked as to who was eligible for membership in SNYC. Ed said, "There isn't any age limit. Anyone who has young, progressive ideas; anyone of any age with ideas that could produce a change in conditions, was eligible for membership."

When Ed Strong said that, I told myself this was the organization for me. I still was not able to read or write easily. But I just stayed around the SNYC and the thoughts of those who were fighting for the rights of the Black and white working class were reflected in my mind as if it were a mirror.

I returned to Birmingham and stayed with the organization, serving along with Mayfield and other friends on the committee which was preparing for the next congress—in Birmingham in 1939. And I stayed with SNYC until it was dissolved in 1948.

In the 1938 period we who were on WPA projects started to organize local Workers Alliance offices in Jefferson County. The national office was in Washington. We set up 27 locals in Fairfield, Westfield, and other little mining towns around Birmingham. When they didn't have meeting halls, they met on the projects in the afternoon after work. In Birmingham we had Local 1, which included unemployed school teachers, ministers, some young lawyers, white-collar and professional people, as well as steel workers and coal miners. It was the largest local in the county.

We met in the Court House. Tom Howell, an ex-coal miner, was elected president; I was vice president; Edwina Collins, a Negro woman, was recording secretary. Room 608, where we met, had a balcony, where the Black members were seated, while the whites sat below in the main auditorium. When we Blacks were elected officers, we had to come down from the balcony and take our seats at the judge's desk along with the rest of the officers. The county officials called the local union leaders into conference on the next meeting night and told them that if Negroes continued to meet with whites on the first floor, we wouldn't be allowed to meet in the court house. When the white union officials came back and reported this, white workers spoke out against the threat, and the union officials were empowered to look for a place where we could all meet together.

They notified us the following Tuesday that we were to go to a vacant hall or 2nd Avenue between 22nd and 23rd Streets, right in the heart of Birmingham and big enough to hold about 300. The hall had two lavatories, one for men and one for women. White men and Black men used one; white women and Black women used the other. In the auditorium, we sat where we could find seats.

Critics from outside the organization tried to break up our union. A few white school-teacher members, too, said, "You white women going to use the same toilet with these colored women? You-all shouldn't do that!"

Ethel Goodman, recording secretary of the Jefferson County Council, came to me, and we agreed to put it to our people something like this: "What is it these outsiders are finding fault about? Are they finding fault with the government for not helping the people to keep from starving? What are they doing to help us get more projects here? What are they doing to get more relief for the unemployed?"

We agreed to say to our people: "Until these critics start fighting and getting some beneficial results for the unemployed, until we see them in action on our side, we won't listen to them. If we're going to get any benefit from what we've been doing, we've got to stick together."

Well, we were able to hold out until May 1, 1939, and in the end it wasn't the critics that closed down the WPA. The workers hadn't yet learned the importance of sticking together regardless of consequences, and when they began to look for other jobs, to a great extent the unity that had been built up between many of the whites and Blacks fell apart.

Nevertheless, race relations began to improve in Birmingham from the time the CIO had begun to organize in 1936.

9
SOUTHERN WORKERS ORGANIZE

I have dwelt on the question of the unity of Black and white unemployed workers because of its great importance in our struggles at this period. White and Black workers were thrown into a position of having to learn that they had the same interests, the same enemy. In the light of their common problems and privations, the whites were better able to see that their claims to innate superiority had no basis—they were in the same bag of oppression and starvation the Blacks had been in all the time.

In Westfield, for instance, out beyond Fairfield, behind the Tennessee Mine Railroad Co., there was a WPA project that was Steel's separate sector for white and Negro workers in that area. The workers were improving school grounds. They were transported by streetcar No. 5, which stopped at the wire mill in Fairfield and then they took trucks from the end of the trolley line to their project. Then suddenly the WPA officials decided they would cut out the trucks and let the workers get to their jobs at Westfield the best they could.

After the workers discussed their complaints for a while, they decided one morning to strike. They marched to the trolley line from the project and then started a sit-in strike at WPA headquarters (known as the Southern Club). They stayed all day and that night, and their wives and relatives brought food to them. Birmingham officials couldn't get them out even when they threatened to call the National Guard and WPA bigshots from

Montgomery. Finally Harry Hopkins sent in a man, and others came in from the state and met with our union committee, and the strike was settled.

Eventually a group of school teachers were fired for being union members. They carried this grievance, along with a number of others that had piled up, to the Workers Alliance headquarters. They met with representatives of WPA in Washington from Harry Hopkins' office, David Lasser, national president of the Workers Alliance, WPA state officials from Montgomery as well as union presidents from various Birmingham locals and from other parts of the state.

The outcome of that free-for-all, heated discussion was general agreement that the workers had a right to belong to a union without any interference by Birmingham WPA foremen or officials. The Alliance grew like a fresh, new plant thereafter, not only in Jefferson County but also in Mobile, Jasper, Gadsen, and Leeds.

Out of this conference there also arose the question of more relief for the unemployed who were not on the projects. There was a committee in Birmingham to handle the grievances of people on direct relief. There were several occasions where workers were evicted from their homes, their furniture put on the sidewalk. Members of the Workers Alliance living in the community reported to the Grievance Committee of Local 1 in Birmingham, and Local 1 sent representatives to find out the facts. The results usually were that these people were taken to the Welfare office, where their cases were presented. On one or two occasions, after Welfare agents had made their investigations, the rent was paid and the Negro tenants were allowed to return to their homes.

Campaigns like these against the anti-labor elements had to be unusually sharp because the foremen just couldn't conceive of organized workers carrying on such activities while they were under the jurisdiction of these

foremen. So it meant war—particularly between the
white foremen and the Black workers. In addition to
feeling that Blacks should not have the right to even talk
about unions, on some of the projects the foremen hired
Black men to inform on the other Negro workers; to find
out what they were talking about; what they said about
the union; what they said about the foremen.

On one occasion, on a project where I was working,
there was a Black stoolpigeon who openly made it known
he was pigeoning for the WPA local officials. As vice-
president of Birmingham's Local 1, and vice-president of
the Jefferson County Council at the time, I got bulletins
from the National Committee of the Workers Alliance on
the developments taking place in the WPA in Washington. If there was going to be a cut or a laying-off of
thousands throughout the nation, this information was
to be found in the bulletin. We got these bulletins before
the work hours in the morning and, after reading them,
we would tell the workers what to look out for.

The stoolpigeon got tired of my exercising this authori-
ty. Even the foremen and the local superintendent, when
they came to work, would walk up and ask, "Well,
Hudson, what's new this morning?" I'd say, "There's
nothing; everything's just the same." Or, if it was important for them to know, I'd say, "Well, if I can have a
few minutes of your time, I want to make an announcement. Something is fixing to happen that we're all much
concerned with," and I would read him one of these
bulletins.

One morning—this was about April 1939—I told the
workers that they were going to cut so many thousands
off WPA throughout the nation. It was announced that
all workers who had been on a WPA project 18 months or
longer must take a 30-day "vacation." This information
was contained in a bulletin from our national headquarters in Washington.

I made the point that the workers must stick together in order to make a comeback; that they must not allow themselves to be torn asunder, because I felt that this was going to be more than a 30-day vacation.

After the announcement, they went to their jobs—picking, shoveling and rolling their wheelbarrows. Later they crowded around and asked me questions. As I was trying to explain, the stoolpigeon, George, stood there looking and listening until he couldn't take it any longer. Finally he said to me, "Let me tell you one thing. I've been hearing you talk on this job for a long time, and me or you, one of us is going to have to leave here, because I ain't going to continue to listen to all this talk about the union and what the union is doing. We're going to find out who is the best down there at the office, you or me." (He meant the Southern Club.)

I told him, "Well, go to it. I don't know where you're getting your help from, but I have the help of thousands of WPA workers, Black and white, men and women, from here to Washington, D.C., in this whole country, behind me, as well as these men on the job. Anything you want to do, you pop your little whip. I'm going to be right here when you get ready to do it."

Everybody burst out laughing and some of the boys stopped talking to him. I told him I'd known a long time that he was a stoolpigeon, always was one, and there wasn't a thing he could do because, in Washington, D.C., the officials recognized the Workers Alliance as the bargaining agent for the WPA workers on government projects. "Your bosses in the Southern Club," I told him, "and the office in Montgomery also have to abide by this fact."

Beginning in the depression period, John L. Lewis had sent in men to organize the coal miners. Although many of the CIO unions had a straightforward position on the rights of Negroes in the mines, the Mine, Mill and Smelter Workers had the most forthright program and fought hardest in the union and in the mines to carry out that program.

Both coal and ore miners had strikes, beginning in 1934 and running through 1938. But from 1934 through 1936, when strikes were called and the miners faced the National Guard on the mountains, there were many times when these mountains became battlefields—they were unlike ordinary strike struggles.

The ore miners—a group of 150 or 200 of them—were blacklisted because they had been active in the unions. They put up a good fight but their appeals dragged on and on. They couldn't get jobs and they went on struggling under the leadership of the Mine, Mill and Smelter Workers until about 1938 when the Labor Relations Board held a hearing in Birmingham. It lasted several months, and I was able to drop in once in a while. Superintendents of some of the mine companies were put on the stand as well as many of the ore miners, who testified that they were beaten up, evicted from their houses and made to suffer other abuses.

The ruling that came out of this hearing was that the miners had to be put back on their jobs and paid for every work day the mine had kept them out, provided they had not been working on other jobs. This was a heartbreaking decision so far as the industrialists of Jefferson County were concerned, particularly for Tennessee Coal and Iron, which appealed the decision to Washington. But they couldn't get the ruling changed. Then they wanted to pay the miners by the month—$30 a month—which the Roosevelt government wouldn't accept either, so they had to pay off the miners in lump sums.

Some of the miners, it was said, drew from three to four thousand dollars. Some bought homes; some bought new cars. They got their jobs back in the mines, with no discrimination. It was especially a great victory for the Black miners, but also for the many militant white workers who had been blacklisted out of the mines along with the Negro workers. The Mine, Mill union and its leadership were branded as a Communist-led union after that great victory for those white and Black workers.

Some time after this, June 1942, I went out to the Jackson founary where they were employing Negroes only in the making of hand grenades, incendiary bombs and torpedoes. I went in as a molder but was put to cleaning coals because, though they needed experienced molders, they didn't have a machine to put me on.

They were paying the molders 48 cents an hour for this government work, day workers 30 cents and iron-pourers 40 cents. And these workers were all protesting that they wanted more money. Since they knew of my role in the Workers Alliance, they came to me about the situation. I told them that the only way they could solve the problem was by organizing.

"So now if you want to do something about organization," I said, "I'm with you, but if you're just talking and grumbling, then I'm not going to have anything to do with it, because I am a new man."

As they went on talking, I went and got five men, handing each of them five cards and taking five myself. This was Monday. Wednesday there was a meeting and all the cards had been signed.

The following Saturday I called another meeting where there were 19 men present. Each of them paid the one dollar fee and we sent away to the Steelworkers of America for a charter. They elected me as president, and other officers too. My name appeared at the head of the charter of Local 2815, United Steelworkers of America, CIO. A few days after our meeting the company fired all the officers of the local except me and the recording secretary. They could not fire me because they needed molders. They planned to fire me later but the company could not catch me organizing on the job.

During the time I headed Local 2815, we were able to get wages raised from 30 to 91-1/2 cents for common labor and $1.04 for molders in our plant. We also got a union shop, the check-off and good working conditions for the whole shop.

The Raymond mine below Bessemer, an ore mine organized by Mine, Mill and Smelter Workers, produced a perfect example of the "tradition" about which an industrialist had spoken at our first hearing in Birmingham. A Black man had never been allowed to run the motors in the mine, although the miner who had seniority for the job was Black. The mine officials opposed putting this man on; the Mine-Mill union leadership demanded that this be done. The klan elements among the union members tried to call a wildcat strike. That morning they formed their picket line, which was supported by the company. They called on the union representatives—Asbury Howard, a Black, Alton Lawrence and Mike Howe, whites, and one or two other militant Blacks.

The union officials told the mine officials, "We didn't authorize this strike, so these men must either go to work or the company must fire them. That's our position." The company told the men to go back to work. The Negro was put on the motor to become the first Black motorman in the mine. But the union leaders, with the threats of the klan hanging over them, had to get permits to carry guns.

Finally, the mine owners, unable to win any other way, closed the mine down, with the excuse that the ore wasn't of good enough quality for war material, and this meant that the miners had to go from place to place looking for jobs. That was how far that company went before it would be outflanked by a Negro.

The builders of the CIO among the Alabama miners included outstanding rank-and-filers who later became Black leaders: Asbury Howard, of Bessemer, for instance (who was put in the city jail later for defending the rights of Negroes to vote); Lewis Tarrant, the first Black man around Birmingham or Bessemer to be president of a local union of whites and Blacks before 1933; Abe Blackman, who became president of the Bessemer Pipe Shop local afterwards; and I, Hosea Hudson, president of Local 2815, United Steelworkers, at Jackson Foundry.

A Black man had to be a militant in the truest sense to head a union local in Alabama, where a sizable element of the membership was made up of Ku Klux Klan.

Henry O. Mayfield, an old friend at the Stockham foundry, now came forward in the Hamilton Slope Coal Mine. But whenever one of the Black workers got up and fought for what he thought was right as a union member in behalf of all the members, regardless of color, he was branded a Communist by the klan elements in the union.

In the CIO organizing drive among steel workers, for example, Mayfield and Joe Howard (who died shortly afterwards), Asbury Howard, along with me and many other Black organizers, went among our people—not only in the mines but in the churches, in the civic organizations, in the voters' league and in whatever activity was going on to help enlist their support.

As president of Local 2815, as well as member of the Birmingham Industrial Union Council, I was put in the position of playing a forthright, militant role both in the organization and in the community. Where the fundamental rights of working people were concerned I had always been militant. I learned to deal with questions involving the welfare of union members, white and

Negro, and I can say that I was respected by the Black community of Birmingham, including civic leaders and trade union members. I will even mention here with some pride that Emory O. Jackson, editor of the Black weekly, *Birmingham World*, named me as one of the men of the year—on the basis of the role I played in the Alabama CIO convention in its discussion and action on the Boswell Amendment.

This was an amendment that would make it more difficult for Negroes to become eligible to vote. I and other leading Black men in Birmingham pointed this out but, somehow, because of my strategic position, I was, in the eyes of the klan elements, a particularly dangerous character.

In 1944, the steel union invited a delegate from Birmingham, England, to Birmingham, Alabama. Carey Hegler, head of the Alabama CIO, at the Industrial Union Council meeting, rose to say that John Henry Jones, a steelworker, was going to be our guest and made a motion that the council appoint a committee to escort Mr. Jones to the various steel plants. It turned out that all the members of the committee were white. A banquet for all the white trade union people to meet Mr. Jones was arranged at the Tutweiler Hotel, but there was no preparation for Negroes to attend that banquet. When they finished appointing all the committees, someone said, "We want Mr. Jones to meet our colored members. Therefore I make a motion that the president be empowered to appoint a committee for that purpose. . . . "

Ben Gage, the president, looked over at me, then at John Hall, of the Packinghouse Workers—a militant rank-and-file Black trade unionist and at another Black member named Jonnie Jones. What would we do about a committee to organize a jimcrow reception for John Henry Jones—we who were constantly fighting against discrimination in the union?

We went off to discuss it and at first I thought I

wouldn't participate. Then I changed my mind and we agreed that I would present a resolution at that reception condemning discrimination. So we proceeded to organize a smoker for our English guest.

Hegler offered any help the state CIO office could give. "You come on up," he said," and we'll get out your cards for you," and our committee wrote the invitation the way we wanted it and took it to his office. But they didn't use a word of our draft; they printed what they wanted on the nice cards with nice gold letters. We accepted them and sent them to everybody, Black and white.

The CIO hall on 19th Street was packed: doctors, attorneys, ministers—Black men and women from all walks of life, the Black leadership of Birmingham.

When John Henry Jones arrived, all the big union leaders—from textile, steel and all the rest—were there, and when they finished the entertainment and just before they got ready to call on the man who was to make the welcoming address, I took the occasion to get up and announce to the chair that we had a resolution I would like to introduce.

Eb Cox, one of the first Negro district representatives of the Steel Union and the only Negro on the staff, was chairman. He tried to keep me from getting the floor, but I succeeded in getting it and I made known the original plan to organize that jimcrow conference. And then I told them about our committee and the resolution of protest, and I called on John Henry Hall, as secretary of the committee, to read the resolution.

After he read it, I seconded his motion to accept it. It was accepted without a single opposition vote. Louis Burnham, head of the Southern Negro Youth Congress, introduced attorney Arthur Shores, already well known as a civil rights lawyer, and he made an address welcoming the guest, after which Carey Hegler introduced the speaker.

John Henry Jones of Birmingham, England, said: "I

don't want to discuss your affairs; that's an internal matter." Then he went on to tell what was going on in his country. But when the question period arrived, everybody wanted to know what they were doing to break down discrimination in England. So, after all, he did get into our affairs, and we had a real discussion on the floor, with various leaders standing up and taking sides.

"Individually, I'm not prejudiced," a member of the Textile Union, which was rampant with white supremacy and discriminatory practices, would say. In many of their shops Negroes were denied the rights to jobs and if they got them it was as sweepers or some other dirty work.

The smoker served the purpose of smoking a lot of white union guys out, though the fight was obviously a long way from being ended. Finally a motion was passed that the resolution be sent to the CIO Council, with a copy to Philip Murray.

When I walked into the council at the next meeting, Frank Parker, the recording secretary, after he had finished reading all the other communications, came over and told me that Ben Gage said if I wanted "this resolution read, I'd have to do it myself."

Black workers sitting around me said, "Hudson, don't bother no more. Just let it go."

I just sat there. Then I said, "Let me handle it."

When they got through all the various committee reports, I made a report on our committee that was organized to handle the smoker. On the basis of its reception, one might say it was a very good report. When I finished, I said, "There was a resolution introduced on that occasion against discrimination and this resolution was unanimously adopted by that body. And this resolution was mailed—as voted—to this council and to Philip Murray."

Then I walked forward to the secretary and I said, "Mr.

President, I'm going to present this resolution now." And I laid it on the table and walked back. Put on a spot among the delegates of the council, Parker had to read the resolution. Then the ball was on again.

I pointed out that undoubtedly there wasn't any conscious desire among union officials to discriminate; but regardless of good intentions, discrimination was going on. There was a big battle, and in the end they had to recognize that the fight against discrimination in that particular union was on and "that guy Hudson" was hard to silence.

In the Industrial Union Council on another occasion, when two Black soldiers came out of the war in 1945, they and their wives were lynched in Monroe, Georgia, I raised the question on the union floor of what the murders of Black fighters against Hitler would mean to the life of the unions and the unity of Black and white. I made a motion that a resolution be passed condemning this act and calling for the arrest and conviction of the criminals. I asked that a copy of the resolution be sent to the U.S. Attorney General, one to the Governor of Georgia and one to Philip Murray, head of the Steel Workers Union.

The white klansmen in the union fought that resolution tooth and nail, but I always was able to get the support of at least a few whites and a large majority of the Blacks. Since Negroes always formed the majority at council meetings, we could put these motions across. Finally, they tried changing the meeting night to Tuesday and every time we took a position against this, they would lose out. It was clear to everybody that I was the main target. "There was only one way to get Hudson and that was to get him out of the council and out of the union."

In October 1947, the *Birmingham Post* carried an article stating that Hudson was suspected of being a member of the National Committee of the Communist Party. The article resulted in the question being raised in the CIO Council. I argued the rights of a U.S. citizen to his convictions, his politics, and his faith, and I wasn't answering any questions about my personal beliefs. During the campaign to get me out of the council, several locals stopped paying their per capita tax. Many whites, including women, took the floor in my behalf. One meeting dragged out till 1:30 a.m., making it necessary to call the police to get one speaker off the floor, which she had held for 30 minutes. They wouldn't let her speak and she wouldn't yield. This fearless leader from the Teachers' Union, CIO, was rudely shouted at and insulted because of her efforts to be heard in the cause of justice.

10

TARGET OF BOSSES AND THE KLAN

At the first state CIO convention I attended (1943), I introduced a resolution in the Constitution Committee to give the CIO Executive Board an additional officer. The president and secretary-treasurer were elected from the Convention at large, but vice-presidents were elected from the various unions affiliated to the councils. Since these delegates came from communities where the unions were dominated by whites, Black delegates were the minority. It was practically impossible to get a Black man elected to any official position in the state body.

The resolution I introduced as a representative of a very young and very small local (built with the help of

John Bedell and many other militant leaders in the Jackson foundry) called for two vice-presidents at large. We hoped that this would give us a chance to elect a Black man to the state executive board. When the resolution was introduced, the paid staff official of the steel union, under the leadership of Noel R. Beddows, fought against it savagely, but after a long discussion, the resolution was passed.

Beddows nominated one of his men from the staff, Ben Gage, and another, named Bertram, both white, but we were able to get Eb Cox, Black, also on Beddow's staff, elected.

This was the first victory. At the next convention of the state CIO, we called a caucus of all Black delegates so that we could pick our candidates; they could come from any union in the state. We agreed to support Asbury Howard of Mine, Mill and Smelter and also another delegate from our caucus, Eb Cox.

When we returned to the convention next morning, we found that the white steel workers had called a caucus of all the members to support a candidate from the caucus—made up of both white and Black delegates—for vice-president-at-large. I was a member of that caucus, too, and I found that the whites wanted to run a candidate that they said would be the "best qualified" in their eyes. This was the Rev. McGruder who, though Black, was strictly a yes-man. I maneuvered to defeat him because we had agreed to support Eb Cox and Asbury Howard. So I rose and asked what union McGruder came from. I said it had been my impression that he worked for the CIO, helping white leaders to organize and contact Negroes, but actually represented no union. They wanted all candidates to be nominated unanimously but I said I would abstain from voting because my question was not answered. Someone from Mine, Mill and Smelter nominated Asbury Howard.

Since I had done all this against the wishes of the klan elements in the Steel caucus, I had put more roadblocks along my path. They had never had a Black worker stand up and speak his mind against what they wanted to do, and they couldn't stomach that. I had to keep much more vigilant against the lies and pitfalls that moved from the union into the shop and the job.

I noted that some of the members of Beddows' staff began to make overtures to John Bedell, my longtime friend and comrade. They tried to buttonhole him and tell him how dangerous I was for the union with my ideas. They told him I was one of the members that Mr. Beddows of the Steelworkers didn't like, and that it would be advisable to get me out and look around for a different Local president.

When Bedell asked who else they would get, they answered, "What about you?" He said, "I wouldn't even try because I'm not able to hold it."

That fall we got ready for the National Labor Board election. The company moved the shop on October 9 back to the old place which, they said, was larger and where they could employ more people.

They laid off about half our members, many of them our best union men, at the Blakely foundry. This was another crippling blow to the local, and especially to me. Many of the laid-off workers were men we could rely on to build the union and who supported me. They sent me down to the Jackson foundry with full intentions of getting rid of me. But I was able to maneuver there and regroup our few remaining members, including Bedell, who had been transferred, too. We were able to reorganize the local.

In February 1944, we had elections, with the AFL claiming a number of our Black union members as members of the Machinists—an all-white union. We were able to win that election and to get the first contract signed on September 8.

In all our struggles, whenever the company had a chance, it would cut off some of the best union members. They put Bedell in to dust on the shake-out—he was suffering from silicosis now—and he had to leave because he couldn't stand it physically. Some of the best men would be caught off guard and the company used everything they could get against them. Somehow I was able to go on working there, and eventually to get the workers organized, to get a signed contract with a check-off, a union shop and, generally, good working conditions in the plant for both Black and white.

The white workers, especially the cranemen, electricians and millwrights, were having a good period. When they didn't have anything else to do, they would stand around and throw the hammers up in the air to see who could catch them. When their work was done, they just amused themselves.

After the death of President Roosevelt in April 1945, Philip Murray was asking for a 25-cent wage increase; 18-1/2 cents was finally granted across the board by Truman. Whites in such categories as mechanics and electricians had got only 7-1/2 cents an hour, we were given to understand. But we found that the company had been giving them two or three cents under the table, without the knowledge of the Negroes. So when we got our 18-1/2 cents they had already been getting nearly 11 cents for some time, and the bosses, not wanting to give them an additional 18-1/2 cents, just gave them the remaining 7-1/2 cents.

Miller, one of the millwrights, asked me how much the Black workers had received, and I told him we got 18-1/2 cents. He said they had received only 7-1/2 cents and I confronted him with the fact that he and the other skilled workers were not in the union. Then he asked could they get the 18-1/2 cents if they joined the union, and I told him if they signed union cards and their names appeared on the check-off list, the union would file a grievance for the rest of the money, although we wouldn't ask for the raise to be retroactive.

I gave him 35 cards and in a few days he brought them back signed and asked for fifteen more. He got those signed, too, and we took them down to the Steelworkers' office.

After we filed a grievance, we found out that the foundry had been giving these men 11 cents in small increases from time to time. But this was contrary to the contract, which provided that any adjustment in wages had to be agreed to by union and management. I put it this way to the company officials—that "with all due respect" they had violated the contract.

The shop superintendent and the vice-president said they'd "be damned" if they'd pay. I said, "Mr. Milton," (the vice-president) "I'll move that this case remain open and that we have another conference in the near future."

They agreed, and at the next conference I called out Ben Gage and Shoemaker from the Steelworkers' district office and, along with our committee, they waited on the company. They had their lawyer (Mr. Young) in on the discussion, pro and con and, finally, he suggested a break for a smoke. They walked outdoors and when they returned after a few minutes, Mr. Young said: "Gentlemen, after discussion, we have agreed we will pay these men the additional 11 cents but we won't make it retroactive."

After all this was done and everything was going fine, the elements who wanted me out of the union began moving around among the whites. First, one of them asked me about a white man being president of the local. I said that the Blacks had built Local 2815 and the membership had elected me president. If they decided they didn't want me any longer and wanted to elect a white, that would be all right with me but I wasn't going to resign in order to turn the local over to a white.

Although they said, "All right, all right!" I could see that they didn't agree with this.

After that time we were involved in various struggles and when they saw they were not winning, they decided to get me out of the union. When the anti-labor Taft-Hartley bill was up for discussion by labor all over the country, Philip Murray sent out instructions for all affiliates to contact officials from the states, the cities and counties to hold meetings to protest against that bill. When the Birmingham Industrial Union Council got the instructions, they tabled it for further reference. But when we came to "new business" I made a motion to carry out Phil Murray's instructions to arrange a mass meeting. They vowed they didn't have money in the treasury. In the floor fight that resulted, we forced them to go on record to call that meeting.

We spent $600 for leaflets and placards and ads in the papers. We got breaks on the radio announcing the meeting. And we had Ben Gage, who had fought so hard against it in the council, helping to fold leaflets for distribution all over the city, with his friends in the council helping him—as well as many paid officials. That was one big setback for the klan.

The only way they could get me was through the shop. They ran an ad in the paper saying that the FBI suspected Hosea Hudson was a member of the Communist Party. They wanted me to make a statement to the council, and I told them that the Constitution of the United States was still the law of the land. Since it gave me the right to think privately in any way I chose, whether about politics or religion, it was my own business, and I wouldn't answer questions for anybody.

That started the ball rolling. When I kept refusing to answer their questions, they sent out an investigator. From November 1947, to mid-March 1948, they tried to get me out of the local and out of the plant.

At a time when the Blacks who worked nights were not

coming to meetings and didn't know what was going on, the whites got the Negroes to sign a petition that the whites told them was for seniority. Actually, they signed their names to a blank sheet of paper and afterward a letter was written in the blank space that said the signers did not want to work with Hosea Hudson in the plant.

When I was called into the office on December 5, 1947, they showed me the list of signatures and read the statement. Then they said they were letting me go because all the machinists and millwrights had decided they were not going to work with me in the plant any longer.

I told them the membership would have the last say about that. I fought this thing, with the support of Local 2815's members, until the third week of March. At that time, after we had a hearing with Judge M. C. McCoy from Tuscaloosa, who was supposed to be an impartial umpire although he was on the company's side, I received a letter saying Judge McCoy had ruled against me.

They gave me that news when I went to the Steelworkers' office. I told them I had lost that battle but I was still fighting that war.

The Black people had not rushed to sign up when World War II broke out. Some Negro newspapers advised us to wait and see what promises the white leaders would make this time. Would they be like those they made to get Blacks to fight in World War I—promises they broke before the returning soldiers could take off their uniforms?

Not all Black men qualified to be soldiers felt that way, but enough did to give Washington a headache, particularly when Hitler attacked England and Japan attacked Pearl Harbor. Many Black people argued that if Hitler won we would be worse off than ever; some said it wouldn't matter much.

A. Philip Randolph, President of the Brotherhood of Sleeping Car Porters, threatened a march of 100,000 Blacks on Washington if the Administration didn't do something to stop jimcrow in job employment, especially in war industries. The march was set for early 1941, and on June 25 of that year the Executive Order was issued by Roosevelt, which supposedly barred discrimination in employment.

Its first act was to set up the Fair Employment Practices Committee (FEPC), which called a hearing in Birmingham in April 1942, in the central post office building. The committee had two Negro members, Chicago alderman Earl Dickerson and Milton Webster of the Brotherhood of Sleeping Car Porters. I was a member of that packed audience for the entire three days the hearings lasted.

There were Black men from the shipbuilding industry in Mobile. A Negro blacksmith's helper testified that he had been "helping" for 17 years though he could do anything the blacksmith could. I heard Dickerson and Webster question the pompous white officials on the stands as if they were in court. He asked why they hadn't changed their personnel practices to give the Blacks opportunities to exercise their knowledge and skills. And their answers circled round and round, "We have a tradition here in the South and we can't violate it." When Dickerson or Webster pinned them down, they said, "We'd have bloodshed."

In Birmingham they had also recently set up vocational training for whites, spending $30,000 for this purpose and, although Blacks made up 35 percent of the population, only $3,000 was allocated to them. And the officials didn't even begin to prepare to do this until they heard the FEPC was coming.

When they were asked why they hadn't spent 35 percent of the money for training the Black population of Birmingham, well, they just couldn't answer. Finally,

Mr. David Sarnoff, president of RCA, said he employed 35,000 workers and he was applying the President's Executive Order. He said he hoped industrialists everywhere would do likewise. Milton Webster told Sarnoff many wouldn't follow his example and, of course, this was what happened.

The hearing caused so much publicity throughout the nation and particularly in the South, that the white supremacist industrialists were put on the spot. So they started a war in the U.S. Congress against the FEPC. The windup of that war found the committee able to function—that is, to just about breathe and even to open and shut its mouth—but it didn't have any teeth. Its power to subpoena, to summon and to question industrialists had been stripped away.

11

CAMPAIGN TO REGISTER AND VOTE

Among the major struggles that were going on in the South between 1944 and 1950 was the fight for the right to vote. In May, 1944, I attended a conference in New Orleans, organized by Rev. Maynard Jackson, an outspoken Black minister from Texas. All Negro organizations and leaders had been urged to come and discuss the Negro people's right to vote. The conference, opening on Friday and going on through Saturday, had 190 in attendance from all parts of the South. I served on the Labor and Industrial Committee, along with Roscoe Dungee, publisher of the *Black Dispatch* of Oklahoma City (I was chairman and Mr. Dungee was secretary). We discussed the role of the Negro—particularly the youth—in labor, and we presented a resolution.

As a result of the two-day discussion, the conference resolved that when we went back home we would organize the Negro Democratic Non-Partisan Voters League on state, county and city levels. John Dobbs of Atlanta, Supreme Grand Master of Negro Masons, took part in a hot debate on the floor between Democrats and Republicans. Dobbs had been a Republican but in the Roosevelt period he had switched to the Democrats. He claimed that the Democrats were doing more for the Black people than the Republicans. An interesting discussion followed.

Before the conference closed, Negro leaders from various parts of the South appeared to tell how they had been flogged by terrorist bands. Leaders of the NAACP came from outlying parts of Louisiana and other sections telling similar stories and bearing their scars as evidence.

We left New Orleans with the intention of organizing Black people in our own communities to fight for the right to vote. Back in Birmingham, I, along with a Mr. Hollins from the Negro Business League—the only representatives from that area who had attended—discussed plans. In the fall of 1944 we called a conference and formed a statewide organization. Delegates from Selma, Huntsville and Tuscaloosa and other parts of the state attended. Emory O. Jackson, Editor of the *Birmingham World,* was acting secretary and we elected attorney Arthur Shores as state president. Then we went out to fight for our voting rights. I represented the Industrial Union Council of Birmingham as well as Local 2815.

At that period the CIO at every one of its meetings and conventions went on record for the rights of its members to vote. But it always seemed that when the officials were talking about its members' rights, they were urging only whites to qualify to vote. This rocked on until the CIO in Alabama, especially around Birmingham, began to try to play a somewhat more active role in politics. During that period it was hard to convince many of the white members that their fight in politics was just as important as their fight on the job for raises and better working conditions. Many kept repeating that they were opposed to taking an active part in politics. They felt that wasn't the function of a union. But to a great extent such notions were shattered in 1944-45. In that period we began being active in the Political Action Committee (PAC) and we were urging locals to set up committees on city- and state-council levels in order to educate members on the importance of qualifying to vote.

One Sunday in Birmingham, CIO officials called a PAC conference which was attended by delegates from locals all around Birmingham and from as far away as Gadsden. Such conferences were repeated on a number of occasions. At the first conference, we elected a committee of seven, with two Negroes (I was one of them) to interview the various candidates for state and national office. The other Black interviewer was a member of the Mine, Mill and Smelter Workers Union.

Eugene Wells was state secretary-treasurer of the CIO and chairman of the PAC committee. They set a date for a meeting at the Thomas Jefferson hotel (in the absence of the two Black committee members) and invited the candidates to be interviewed so that we could find out what their opinions were with regard to labor. They had the interview with the candidates, but the Black committee members hadn't even been notified of what was going on.

At the county-wide PAC conference in Birmingham, committees were asked to report on that meeting (this was a big gathering, with delegates from all the affiliates). The committee's report on the candidates' attitude was fine, but we Blacks who had been elected by the general conference and ignored in the interviews, tried to take the floor. Chairman Carey Hegler tried every possible maneuver to prevent this. Every time anyone else would raise his hand (even though mine was still up) he would recognize the other person and avoid looking at me.

After they had heard the various discussions, they made a motion to accept the committee's findings and the candidates recommended by the committee. All the whites were yelling, "Call the question!" so the motion was passed—without our having had a chance to speak.

After their "victory" I took the floor and requested a point of special privilege. They allowed me this and I made known the situation—not only that we Blacks hadn't been notified and that the committee had reported without consulting us but that they had denied the floor to me and had proceeded to appeal to the delegates to go back to the locals and appeal for funds to support the candidates.

This was unacceptable inasmuch as I represented not only my local but many Black people who were not in the local union. Many Black people who were leaders in their communities, as well as members of the rank and file, accepted my leadership. Since I had been denied the rights of the floor and the right to interview the candidates, as a Black man seeking to get the support of Black voters for labor's candidates, I wanted to make it known that I wasn't going to ask my local for a dime to support these candidates. Nor was I going to use my influence to get votes among Negroes for these candidates.

"I will leave it up to the Black people to use their own judgment," I concluded. "I'm not going to rally any support among the members of the Jackson foundry." (At that time we had 590 members under my leadership.)

At the 1946 Atlantic City Steel Workers CIO Convention, when the questions of PAC and the rights of members to vote were being discussed, I took the floor and spoke on the right-to-vote resolution, raising sharply the importance of the whites going back to their locals and giving every possible assistance to their Black members in getting them qualified to vote. The Negro union members—and the whole Negro people—would then support the labor candidates, because what was good for the laboring Negroes was good for the whole Negro people. They were on the bottom rung and needed all the help they could get in winning certain rights by legislation as well as certain rights in the union.

The 2,600 delegates attending the convention responded with generous applause. Beddows, who was there as the district director from the Birmingham Steelworkers, finally got around to the Black delegation, recognizing Blackman, from the Bessemer Pipe Shop local. When he took the floor, he said: "I defy any man to say that the Negro has not made progress under the CIO in Alabama." In order to get his full statement mailed to me, I left my name and address, along with a dollar. A few weeks later I received the convention minutes and had a chance to read all my remarks and right after them, Abe Blackman's. I realized then for the first time that he had actually been speaking against me (he had a membership of about 1800 in his local).

I took those minutes to some of his most active Negro members to read, letting them see both my statement and his. The dissatisfaction brought about in his local by his remarks caused him eventually to resign. These Black steel workers pointed out they didn't need leaders who would make remarks against their interests when they had sent him to speak for them.

Meanwhile, during that summer in Birmingham, the Board of Registrars opened on every first and third

Monday, especially for veterans to go down to qualify for voting. I took down six young Black veterans, one of whom was my son, and another a minister. I stayed with them all day, having prevailed upon them not to leave but to stick it out.

We looked at the long line of Black people and phoned Rube Farr's office (he was on the staff of the district director of the Steel Union) and reported that they were not receiving Negroes; that they were putting whites through and letting Blacks stand in line. So he sent two white men I didn't know, but I found out who they were by listening to them.

They called the chairman of the Board of Registrars outside into the hallway, and I got close to them where I could hear their conversation. One said to the Chairman of the Board of Registrars (a very old man), "We didn't come down here to change your rules or to change your practice. We came because we were told to come, because we had to come, and we want to make it known to you that we are with you 100 per cent. And you can rest assured we aren't trying to change any of your rules."

I went back to the telephone and called Farr. I told him those men "don't mean any good." And I repeated what I had overheard.

Emory O. Jackson of the *Birmingham World* was present at that time, as was the Secretary of the Birmingham branch of the NAACP. The matter of Black voter registration was one that united various viewpoints in the Negro community.

I don't know what was going on behind the scenes but the registrars must have wondered why so many "Negro leaders" were sticking around and continuing to urge those Blacks to stay there and get registered. All six of the young men finally got through and were interviewed by the registrars. All six got their certificates in the mail a few days later.

The struggle for the right to vote continued through

the late 1930's and the 1940's, especially for the Black
young men who had fought against Hitler. It was conducted under the sponsorship of the Southern Negro
Youth Congress which, right after World War II (with
Henry Mayfield leading) conducted 150 Black veterans to
the Jefferson County Court House to demand the franchise.

The veterans had called a conference to consider their
problems: vocational training, jobs, housing, the right to
vote—all under the leadership of the Southern Negro
Youth Congress in Birmingham. Truman had just followed Roosevelt in the presidency and I heard many
leaders from Tuskegee Institute, as well as others, saying we would have to wait and see what this new
president would do about carrying on the Roosevelt
program. At that time we were going around in circles
and many were expressing the idea that Negro veterans
should try to solve their problems by starting their own
small businesses.

Here were young men just out of the army and not yet
able to buy clothes to wear (there was a shortage of
civilian clothing, especially business suits), and they
were being told to become business men. At the conference of the Southern Negro Youth Congress I became
vexed with such talk; I said they were living in an unreal
world—not in this world where tough problems existed
for the Negro vet. There was one thing that couldn't be
overlooked: we *did not* have a Roosevelt in the White
House any more, and in order to get the concessions that
were so badly needed, we would have to organize around
a program in the interests of the veterans. We would
have to enlist the support of all possible sources and
especially of organized labor.

After my remarks, a Mr. Campbell, of Tuskegee's
Agricultural Department, addressed the conference.
"You know I am at a loss," he said. "I don't know where to

start. I've listened to many different speakers, but this young man from organized labor has really got me so I don't know where I am."

Out of that Black veterans' conference, many efforts began to be made by them to secure decent conditions. Louis Burnham and his co-workers in leadership of the Southern Negro Youth Congress initiated the idea of the conference and the movement that followed when they sent 150 Black vets marching on the Jefferson County Court House.

And right after this phase of the struggle began, the FBI got busy investigating and intimidating the leaders and members of the organization. One of them was an insurance agent, one a school teacher. When Black people begin to struggle seriously the FBI starts snooping around, buttonholing people and pointing out who is "dangerous."

At the conference called in Columbia, S.C., in 1946, by the Southern Negro Youth Congress, at the Negro university in that town, there were delegates not only from all walks of life in the South but also from Africa, Asia, Europe and all the Americas. The leadership of the SNYC, because of its militancy and the respect it enjoyed in the Black community, was one of "Bull" Connor's [Birmingham's Police Commissioner, who was to reach the peak of notoriety in the 1963 civil rights demonstrations] special targets.

Columbia certainly wasn't picked for the convention because it was near the home of James F. Byrnes, an outstanding Dixiecrat and segregationist, who generally spewed forth racist poison. But it was a convenient location, and we had such important questions on our agenda as vocational training and the right of Negro youth to hold any job for which they were qualified. The foreign youth, particularly youth from countries dominated by U.S. imperialism, showed some interest in the fact that James F. Byrnes was Franklin Roosevelt's Secretary of State and that he lived nearby.

At this conference the SNYC went on record in favor of a one-day work stoppage, known as "The Stoppage for the Right of Negro Youth for Jobs." In the discussions, the young people showed that they were deeply concerned over the fact that their rights to recreation in city parks were regularly and brazenly denied. They felt that nobody was doing anything against the denial of elementary citizenship rights and that it was time the Negro youth themselves spoke up. The convention also specifically challenged Byrnes, condemning him for his anti-Negro actions in Washington.

It was because SNYC played such a militant role in Birmingham and throughout the South from 1939 to 1948 that klan elements and other white-supremacists increased their attacks.

During the early days of the war period, when Jim Jackson was in the army, and his wife, Esther, the Executive Secretary, was busy in the SNYC, there was an article in a Birmingham newspaper actually calling for lynch terror against Mrs. Esther Cooper Jackson. It urged such elements as the Ku Klux Klan to go down to the Negro Masonic Temple and look up this "shaggy-haired half-breed sitting in the office there." Such attacks only strengthened the support of Negro youth —and of the Negro people in general—for the Southern Negro Youth Congress.

Attacks on SNYC, however, came not only from what we have called klan elements; they came also from such whites as the District Director of the CIO, the CIO State President, and the District Director of the Steel union. Led by such men as Beddows and Mitch in their redbaiting of the SNYC, they were aiding and abetting the work of those elements of the klan who were in and around the unions. But the seeds sowed by the organization during this period when the CIO in general had a progressive program—particularly the leadership of the Mine, Mill and Smelter Workers around Bessemer—are still proving they were good if we judge by the fruit still growing from them today.

12

MY EDUCATION CONTINUES

In looking back at the decade 1934–44, it was really in the period after the 1936 election that Roosevelt took the New Deal path—the era that was marked by such legislation as the Wagner Labor Relations Act, the Wages and Hours Act and the Fair Employment Practices Act (FEPC).

In our Party unit we studied these matters in the light of Marxism-Leninism, and even with our limited education we understood what was to be gained through the New Deal. I myself enjoyed many opportunities I would never have dreamed of at an earlier period in Birmingham, for instance, being able to talk about the union on the job, to talk to workers about various issues affecting their interests around the shop.

After the National Labor Relations Board was set up, we workers could discuss even more freely with the others in the plant how the changes that had come about would affect us and what action we could take to make sure we got the full benefit of the New Deal period.

Not that it was clear sailing, by any means. There were all kinds of people, sympathetic people, who would come to Birmingham wanting to know what they could do to help the Party. There was Paul Crouch, for example, teaching classes in the history of the Communist Party of the Soviet Union. It was the first time we were able to open a Party office and have classes like this.

Paul Crouch's son was in the hospital and needed blood. Party members went to the hospital and gave the blood needed to save his kid. We looked upon Crouch as a real friend and a leader of the Party—not knowing we were really dealing with a man who was later to become a stoolpigeon.

In Birmingham, the Party had pushed forward in the face of all the terror facing it. When Negroes were arrested they were not merely taken to jail, they were whipped and left for dead in the cornfields. Frank Harvey, a YCL member, was whipped unconscious and left for dead, by the Ku Klux Klan, it was said. And in 1935 Willy Foster, representing the ILD in Birmingham, went to investigate the terror against members of the Sharecroppers Union and was never seen or heard from again. All we know is that he went to Selma, Alabama, where, some 30 years later, Alabama law-and-order enforcers mobbed and assaulted Dr. King's nonviolent marchers, and members of the KKK murdered Mrs. Viola Liuzzo, a white civil rights worker.

It was in 1935, during the Sharecroppers Union struggles that we heard many reports that Negroes were kidnapped from the fields in broad daylight and taken away, never to be seen again.

Among the many people I met and talked to, there was a visitor from the Soviet Union who wanted to see me. This was in 1946. I told Tex Dobbs, who headed the Civil Rights Committee, to bring him out to my house. Tex Dobbs, the Soviet visitor, his interpreter, and a government man, came out. The Russian was a writer, by the name of Ilya Ehrenburg. They told me he was one of the most important writers of the Soviet Union.

He had been around Birmingham and met members of the city Chamber of Commerce, union officials, even some of the big industrialists, and some of the prominent whites. And now he was at my two-room wooden house because he wanted to meet a "typical steel worker."

We talked about 30 minutes or so, but the more I told him about how Negroes lived in Birmingham, the more questions he asked. He wanted to know why I was living in that kind of house. I told him I had to live where my wages would let me live.

Well, I told him so much about the Black people in the South, the steel workers and others, about police brutality and lynchings and jimcrow—that his government companion got restless. He got Ehrenburg into the yard and kept saying, "Come on, let's go!" We were ready to go on talking and his interpreter was ready to translate, but we walked out and stood on the steps, then walked out on the grounds. But the government man had gone out to the street, because the conversation was too hot for him—he couldn't stand hearing it. And I just went on talking and the interpreter went on translating. . . .

I learned later that it came out in *The New York Times* that Ehrenburg had made a statement that among all the people that he met in Birmingham the only one who knew the conditions and had the answers for the problems of his people was a Negro steelworker.

Because of that statement, white professors came to the SNYC office in the Masonic Temple from the school at Mount Eagle, Tennessee to meet me. I had all kinds of invitations; they wanted to ask all sorts of questions. But I couldn't spare the time from my work in the union and I had no wish to become a big shot. I felt this way all through my life in the unions—I wanted to remain a steelworker, a union leader who stood up for what I believed was the right way to fight for the masses. I took the same hardships as the workers did; I did my suffering the way they did theirs. I did not want to be a yes-man for money.

Let me tell you, for instance, a little about my experience with the FBI. When "Bull" Connor started his offensive against me, John Bedell, Henry Mayfield, Sam Hall, Andy Brown and several others in Birmingham, we had had to leave our homes for personal security, not because we were criminals violating any law. Every where I went I was dogged by the FBI. If I stayed overnight at a friend's home, in the next few days the FBI would be there. They would tell my friends I was a criminal, a murderer.

After I had lost my jobs both at the foundry and as president of the union in 1948, the first place I went to work at was the Miller foundry in Birmingham, which made machine parts for the International Harvester Company. The foreman at Miller's knew me and told me there was a job it seemed that no one could make and he wanted me to "give it a trial." It was a part that had to be made very smooth—a piece that went into a corn-dropping machine. I went on this machine with two other Black men. I worked on it Thursday and Friday until noon, when the cupola burned out and we all had to knock off.

I went back the following Monday and worked until noon, when they came and told me that they would have to lay off some men. Since I was one of the newest, they were sorry but I would have to go to the office and get my money. If they found they needed me, they'd send for me.

I went to the pay office; I had worked one full day and two half-days and when they paid me I noticed that they handed me five $10 bills, one $5 bill and ten cents—a total of $55.10. I don't know how they made the mistake, but I just took it and walked off. I felt it was the responsibility of the company, the paymaster and the timekeeper—it wasn't my responsibility to keep the time.

I then went to the Rex foundry in Irondale outside of

Birmingham. The foreman asked if I was a molder and said they had a job—to make the top of the mold. When he asked me if I thought I could make it, I said I would be willing to try. It meant making a large radiator in the form of a coil, in circles, something about four inches inside. I was told the order was for 50,000, and they were to be made for a housing project being built by the great baseball pitcher, Dizzy Dean, in Chicago. If I could cover up 50 a day, I'd have my day's work.

They had six men on that job: one man who made the bottom and his helper; one who made the core and his helper; and I made the top with my helper. We started to work at seven a.m. The core-setter was white and the fellow who was making the bottom (which we called the drags) was Black. The rest were all Black. By noon I'd have covered up 50 molds. And the little boss would walk by and I'd ask, "How's it going?" and he'd say, "All right, all right." And we poured off those 50 molds and at about 2:30 we were ready to go home. They were paying me $1.25 an hour. And my day was made. The little boss would come by every morning and he'd feel the facing in the closed space next to my pattern on the machine, and I'd say, "How is my facing?" "You're doin' fine," he'd say.

One morning—I had been working about a month—he walked by and he didn't put his hand in the facing. I looked at him, watching his every move. He didn't look at me. I got suspicious, but I went on working. He didn't come around again all morning.

So we put up that day's work, poured off our molds and so forth. Nobody said anything, and I went home. The next day I was at my place, ready for work, when he came to me.

"Hudson, you know, we're going to have to close this job down. We've been shipping these castings to Chicago by airplane, they were in such a rush. We haven't got any pay for them, so we're going to have to shut down until he sends us a check. You go and get your money, and you call us and we'll let you know when you go back to work."

I was suspicious, but I went home. I called every few days and they told me they were not ready to work yet. I finally decided I'd catch the bus and go out there.

When I got there they had men making the job, so I walked in and said to the foreman, "I see you got started again." He said they had tried to get over to me but couldn't find me so had to get another man.

"We're doing pretty good so we'll let him try it out a while. We'll let you know when we need you again."

Of course, I never heard from them, and I knew that someone was moving around behind me and would try to rob me of any job I undertook. I decided to quit trying to work in a shop. I had saved a little money and I went to New York's Union Square and bought about $15 worth of razor blades. They were good blades, known as CANCO, and I got permission to sell them wholesale throughout the South.

When I went to Memphis, one of my first stops, I made friends there among the union members. I went around the union halls and sold razor blades to the union members. I wasn't making a living, but at least I was trying to do something.

My last visit to Memphis had been in 1951, after I had to leave Birmingham. I was in the home of one of my union friends one afternoon sitting and reading the paper when they called me for dinner. As we finished our meal and I walked back into the living room, I saw two white men coming up the steps. They didn't look right to me, and I decided to walk back to the kitchen. One of them followed me in, calling "Earl, Earl."

I walked out to the back porch and he followed me out, continuing to call "Earl," and since my name wasn't Earl I didn't answer. Eventually I turned around. "You calling me?" He said he was. I told him I was not Earl. He asked me what it was and I told him my name was Hosea Hudson. He said, "Come on back and let's sit and talk."

Since I had begun handling the razor blades, I had become somewhat active in the work of the Negro Masonic order. I had set up lodges when people wanted them set up. (I was the Supreme Grand Deputy Master Mason.) I had all my papers with me as we took our places there in the sitting room. They wanted to know if I had anything to identify myself and I showed them my credentials to sell the razor blades. Then they asked how I found out about that company in New York. I told them I was a union man and in New York I met some people who knew about the blades. When they asked me for further identification, I pulled out my Masonic card and asked if that would help, and also my identification as Supreme Grand Deputy Mason. One of the men said, "That's all right."

He showed me his FBI identification. They were looking for somebody else; they didn't know who I was. I gave them my old address in Birmingham—the one from which "Bull" Connor had run me out—and they finally left.

I asked my friend whether he thought I should remain at his house. He said, "I don't really know what to say." Finally he said I could stay for the night, but he phoned another friend, then got me a taxi so that I could look for this address on the far outskirts of Memphis. I went out there but couldn't find it. Then I remembered a friend who lived on another side of the town, and the taxi finally got me there.

When I got to the house I learned that the husband was dead and that he had left a widow and ten children. The mother had gone to her club meeting but all the children were at home and they told me to wait. They ranged from six to about eighteen.

The Chicago train that I thought I would take had left,

so I called the YMCA but it was crowded because there
was a Negro insurance-men's convention in Memphis.
Eventually, the mother came home and said I could stay
there. She slept with the children and gave me her bed.

The next afternoon, the man at whose house I had
stayed originally sent someone to tell me not to leave.
"The fellows" had called Birmingham and had been told
who I was, and that night at about one o'clock two
carloads of white men had come to his house looking for
me.

While this messenger was talking, telling me not to
leave, a thought shook me telling me to go. The wife of
my friend had washed and ironed my white shirt. A train
left at seven p.m. and it was already past six. The man
who had brought the message kept saying over and over,
"Don't you leave." I said I hadn't killed anybody or
robbed a train. And my instinct kept telling me to go. I
asked them to get me a taxi and I picked up my suitcase
and a batch of razor blades I was carrying.

I asked the driver whether he could make the railroad
station by seven and he said he could. We got in the car
and made off. I arrived at the station just four minutes to
train time. I ran to the ticket office and bought my fare,
rushed out and just made it into the train. It seemed to
me there were white men standing at the gate watching
everybody.

In Chicago I found some friends, including Sam Hall
and his wife, who had moved here from their home in
Birmingham. They were running away from Bull Connor, too. Among the old friends I met there was a man
who was going back South to New Orleans by way of
Memphis, and when I had told him my story he said he
would stop by the house of the woman where I had stayed
and find out what happened.

She told him to tell me not to come back that way. Ten minutes after I'd left, she said, two carloads of FBI men arrived, searched the place and asked questions. She put up with all the questioning, she said, because the longer the FBI stayed, the farther away I was getting.

What happened that same night, earlier, at the first house was that the FBI agents arrived and found that I had gone. Knowing that a last bus was leaving for Chicago at two a.m., they rushed to the bus station. They saw a large Black man sitting in the bus station. The city police, who were with the agents arrested him, took him into an alley, and beat him up, breaking his arm.

It turned out that he was the preacher of three churches around Memphis. His congregation and the Black community protested, raised a big to-do about it but they got no satisfaction so far as I have been able to learn.

It has been my experience that the FBI gets the city police to do its dirty work for them. If I had not followed my intuition and stayed away from the bus station that night it is hard telling whether I'd be living today.

Yes, they were always on my trail like a bunch of hounds. As recently as the Civil Rights March on Washington in 1963, when I could hardly walk because of arthritis in both my knees, they came and asked me why I didn't go on the march. I told them I didn't think it necessary for me to go; now that the young people were taking over, I was going to sit back and let them carry on because I and others had sowed the seeds.

They said, "That's right, Mr. Hudson. You have done enough. Do you know we would like to talk with you sometime?" When I said I had nothing to tell them, they said that Mr. Hoover would be glad to have me cooperate and would make it worth my while.

When I asked them how they figured I would betray

the friends who gave me bread when they, the FBI, were running me out of jobs, they said, "Oh, no, we don't want that!"

I told them that after the *Birmingham Post* in big headlines reported that the FBI said they suspected me of being a member of the Communist Party, I had lost my job, indirectly lost my family, and had many times come close to losing my life because the FBI followed me around, telling people I was a murderer, a criminal.

"Everywhere I've gone since 1948, when I came back two or three years later, people would tell me you had been there with my pictures, telling them what a dangerous character I was.

"I know this is your job; you're working for your boss and have to do what he orders. I am not going to cuss you out, but I don't have to give you any information."

It is my conviction that the fish of the sea, the rabbits in the brier patch, the squirrels in the trees and the deer in the meadows have better protection in state and federal law than our Black people have. There have been people sent to prison every year for shooting squirrels. But how many lynchers have been sent to prison?

So I have asked and I still ask how this can be the "American Way of Life"—government of the people, for the people and by the people? All the lynchings, all the brutality and discrimination the Black people have suffered and are suffering—what can these have to do with democracy?

As things are moving today there must be a change, and that change must be one that improves the lot of the masses of our people. The only way we can bring that about is through education and organization. For myself, I found political guidance in the Communist Party toward united action with all the people.

13

OBSERVATIONS AND TRIBUTES

When we talk about education, we have also to understand the people who didn't go to school but who are well equipped mentally—they just need to be set in motion. Once they get the idea, they move. I fully believe this because it has been verified by my own experience. The Party taught me that the masses of people must be educated politically, through struggle—even the struggle to write a postcard, a letter; sacrificing to buy reading material and struggling to read it. Struggles to achieve people's day-to-day needs are the basis of political education.

On one occasion, Ben Davis, Jr., who later became the first Black Communist Councilman in New York City, called together about ten Negro schoolteachers. He wanted me to lead the discussion on political economy. I was hesitant because I didn't think I could talk, but after I got started I forget who I was talking to; I just thought of what I was talking about. When the teachers began to discuss my remarks, they were very appreciative.

I would never have been able to express myself if it hadn't been for the Communist Party. So when I hear people refer to Party members as "subversives," "spies," and so on, I realize they don't know what they're talking about—or they do know and are using their lie as a weapon. What I was told and what I learned the hard way was that frame-ups were constantly set up because there was no other way to keep the Black people down.

When Bedell and I, in 1932, began to move, to change and to get to new people, we were on relief; everybody was unemployed, so nobody was any better off than anyone else. We would organize a committee in the community to go down and get food for the people. The Party taught us how to do that.

On the basis of the role we played in that early period, we were prepared to play a greater role in major struggles—like organizing the CIO, particularly in steel. I developed a bulldog determination not to be pushed down, so I was able to stand up and speak out. That was what helped me organize 500 workers in Local 2815 in the Jackson foundry, Black and white; to get three contracts signed, with wage increases, seniority, vacations with pay, a percentage on all jobs, with basic pay and premiums on the shakeout. It was stated by the union leaders that the Jackson Foundry Steel Lodge was one of the best organized and had the best conditions of all the union locals around Birmingham. I give credit to the Party; if it had not been for the Party, I wouldn't have known how to talk up, let alone how to organize.

And again, thinking of the Scottsboro Case, we were able to have an influence on a lot of things in Birmingham as a result of our learning how to organize the masses and apply mass pressure.

We all learned to write postcards and letters of protest, to put out leaflets—in other words to educate ourselves in action. At our meetings we had reports and checkups—what literature we had sold, how people had reacted to it and to our paper. A friendly competition developed, as everyone wanted to do something he could report. The people began to look forward to hearing from us; they wanted to know what was going on. So we made friends and broadened our relationship with the workers.

We continued the work in the church. We'd talk about

something we had read in the papers; we would get up a discussion, get people to talk pro and con—all the while educating the Black people and educating ourselves. Once they recognized that we understood what was going on, they would come around to hear what we had to say. We read, because we had to in order to stay ahead.

One afternoon a group of us were discussing democratic rights for Negroes. A woman asked if we thought our people could gain their democratic rights in this present society. Nat Ross, a white Communist from the North, said, "If you could begin to organize sufficient mass pressure and public opinion, you would be able to gain a lot of rights long before you get socialism."

When he was asked, "What is this democracy you-all are talking about?" he said it meant the right to vote, to serve on juries, to hold public office, to participate along with all other citizens in politics.

We talked about wars, including imperialist wars for the conquest of markets, and revolutionary wars where colonial peoples struggled to free themselves from domination both by the big imperialist powers and the puppet leaders in their own countries.

Another experience that was tied in with my friendship with Ben Davis comes to mind. He was driving in a car from Atlanta, where he was defending Angelo Herndon, to New York, and he picked me up along with two or three others who were working among the Black Belt sharecroppers. That was the first time I had been able to get out of Alabama and Georgia. Even the Carolinas looked like a new world. And when I got up around Washington and from there to Philadelphia and saw all the monuments to the warriors of the revolution, that was a sight for my eyes!

On our way to New York, I was able to see some historic battlegrounds of the Civil War. Ben and the others were discussing how the South nearly whipped the

North and how far North they had marched. Before that I had thought the only fighting took place in the South.

In New York, I went down around the waterfront, down to the southern end of Broadway and saw a picnic ship. It was the first time I had ever seen a ship. It was on July 4, 1933, as cold as October, and some men were wearing overcoats. I had on light clothes, but I was willing to suffer from the cold because of the excitement of seeing so many things for the first time.

I went back South with even more determination. I told Bedell, Will Carroll and Joe Howard about what I had seen in New York and we continued working in the organization with even more encouragement and better spirit. In Atlanta at that time, Fulton County Prosecutor Boykin put on a drive against the ILD and the Party leaders, so that they had to leave the area for a time. The rank and file was left to itself. Someone was needed to keep contact with the people, so they sent me to Atlanta. I went to the only person I knew there, Ben Davis. He was a lawyer, had been to college, and yet he was a common man, a man that didn't feel he was superior. He greeted me like an old friend, and we talked, he and his law partner, John Gates, and his father, Ben Davis, Senior, who was the editor of the *Atlanta Independent*, a leading Black Republican and a militant fighter for Black people's rights.

Ben gave me the names of some Black people I could go to see in a place called Peoplestown. I began to make friends with them; told them why I had come, that I was sent to see them because some of the leaders had been arrested and some had disappeared. I wanted to find out how they were getting along and to let them know they were not alone. They told me they had still another friend on the West Side, by the name of Weaver. I went to see him but met his brother-in-law instead and was able to gather a little group of people together.

Atlanta's Textile Workers Union was on strike; the

Party had distributed a leaflet pointing out some of the fundamental weaknesses among the textile workers and what had to be done to strengthen the union. Two young white women textile workers were distributing leaflets. They were arrested and put in jail. The ILD wrote leaflets explaining the situation and defending the women. I called a meeting on the West Side, with Moldens, Matthews, Weaver and a few other members. We discussed the leaflet, and it was agreed that everybody should participate in the distribution. I told them how to go about it, but I was careful not to push it down their throats. The main thing was that the leaflet had to get to the people.

The difference between us was that I was from Birmingham, home of the coalminers and the steelworkers, and the Atlanta people were still something of the white-collar type of workers who could do a lot of talking but didn't like to get out into the struggle. Their objection was that they couldn't work in Atlanta like we could in Birmingham; Boykin was in Atlanta and the police were around everywhere. Well, I led the discussion that night, and we couldn't agree. I even described how we could fold the leaflets one by one and put out ten; I told them how important one leaflet could be if it got into the hands of even one person who would show it to two or three others. Maybe as many as ten would see it, and imagine what ten could do in a neighborhood! But my friends wouldn't even put out ten apiece.

I wouldn't push it any further but I began to study how I could get around the problem. I was running up against something I had never experienced in Birmingham. So I dropped the idea and took the leaflets home with me. Each person there took just one apiece. I went down to the office, saw Ben, and told him what I was up against.

He said, "I'll tell you what we'll do. You go back and call a meeting. Set a time as soon as possible, since these girls are still in jail, and tell them I'll be down there."

So I went to see them one by one and the first I saw was Weaver. I told him Ben wanted to have a meeting and he picked a night. I got him to agree to see the others with me. We didn't have any trouble with those in Peoplestown—actually, of course, they were workers, too, but they considered themselves superior since they were insurance office workers, contractors, carpenters, and so on. We got the meeting set, and I notified Ben when and where and he said he would be there.

Of course, I brought back my bundle of leaflets. After the discussion, Ben told them about the arrest of the two young women and how they'd been in jail ever since. He told them about the legal status of the case, what the ILD was doing to get them out on bail, and so on. Afterwards, I spoke about the importance of the leaflets, saying it would in itself help to break down the prosecution if the police saw these leaflets appearing throughout the city. It would weaken their hand; make it easier to get the high bail reduced. We had had the leaflets several days, I said; the girls were in jail, and we were sitting around free and so afraid we couldn't even put out a leaflet. In opposition, Matthews and Weaver and Moldens and two or three others tried to take the same position as they had before.

Ben sat and listened to everything, let everybody talk. When they finished, he got up and said, "Comrades" (he could cuss, and on this occasion he did but I'm leaving that out), "What are you all talking about? I listen to you and I don't fathom what you mean. First, let me tell you something. You-all look on Hosea here as being just an ordinary worker because he does not have a schooling like we've had, hasn't the vocabulary we have, so you don't have to respect him. I want to tell you right here and now that I have a very high respect for Hosea because he can teach us all something. He has had a proletarian education, which we don't have. We had a bourgeois education, but Hosea has a Marxist-Leninist education. We have only what the capitalist class taught us in their schools."

They sat there, with their mouths open.

"I'm going to take out some leaflets, and I want every one of you to take some of them tonight and put them out. From here on in, whatever Hosea suggests, you sit down and discuss it and then each of you carry out the assignment when you come to an agreement. You must discipline yourselves to respect leadership, and we all have to respect Hosea's leadership."

Everyone then took leaflets and distributed them. Not only that, but we were going to have another meeting where everyone would come back and report the results and what they had heard among the people about the leaflet.

From then on I didn't have any trouble after we sat down and agreed on what we would do.

I always enjoyed working with Ben and I felt that we had a partnership when I was in his company, never the feeling of being an inferior in the presence of a high superior.

During this period the Party was raising the question of the equalization of education for Blacks and whites. It went to great lengths to get the figures that showed how much money was appropriated for each white child's education compared with the amount spent for each Negro child's. It went on to emphasize full economic, political and social equality and rights for the Negro people.

I was told by a Birmingham Negro that white politicians had called together leading Negroes to set up a Negro Democratic Club. The whites were to charter this club under the Alabama Democratic Committee and allow it to hold meetings and have its own officers. The sole purpose would be to get out the Black vote. My informant told me the whites wanted to do this because the Communists were agitating among the "less fortunate" Negroes and the whites were afraid the Black masses as a whole might get interested.

The Registration Board wouldn't qualify over 50 Negroes a year, and these were to be the people that the Negro Democratic Club would recommend. They were not going to allow any working-class Negroes; only the "better class" would register. (It turned out that the man who told me all this was the president of that Negro Democratic Club.)

As a result of the continuous demand for the Negro's right to vote and hold office, we were able under the Party's leadership to break through here and there and to change the picture a little. The Scottsboro Case gave us a chance to raise basic demands, including the right of Negroes to serve on juries like those that were hearing the Scottsboro Case.

We were also raising the question of unemployment and social insurance for all unemployed and part-time workers and the question of low-rent government housing, so that low-paid people could have decent shelter. Both of these issues were of particular appeal to the poor Black community. There were many discussions and some arguments on the streets about how, or if, any of this could ever come about. It was when Bedell, Joe Howard and others were working with the people on welfare projects, digging in the red hills around Birmingham, that old-age pensions came to pass.

At one of the first meetings of Party representatives in the South, in Birmingham, I first met Angelo Herndon. I also met Otto Hall, a Black district organizer from Georgia. Herndon, Hall and others from Georgia had just had a big victory—the march of the unemployed on Atlanta's City Hall, demanding more relief for the unemployed. Everybody was enthusiastic, congratulating the Atlantans for their success. But the next week, back in Atlanta, Angelo Herndon was arrested at his post-office box as the leader of that noted demonstration. The charge was insurrection—and this was, of course, the beginning of the famous Herndon Case.

Ben Davis was his first attorney in Atlanta.

As I reflect on the Party as a teacher and guide, I think of the coal and ore mines of Alabama in the New Deal days. Before the union moved there, the miners went to work before daybreak and got home after dark. At the end of the week they were paid at the rate of $2.50 a day. Sometimes their expenses for sharpening their tools in the mines and buying the powder and the caps for blasting would run so high that the men wouldn't have anything left for food. They'd have to go back to the mine commissary. That was the life of a man in the Lewisburg coal mines, as I knew it through personal contacts.

When the union moved in under John L. Lewis's leadership, the battle started. These miners were all ready to go and the going was tough at the beginning. Men trained to think along Marxist-Leninist lines were among the rank-and-file strike leaders. A local was set up among Sariton coal miners; others followed—Lewisburg, Sloss Sheffield, Hamilton & Slope, TCI, and so on. And the struggles around the miners' wages and other grievances were on.

The miners were faced on the picket lines by the company's armed deputies. Later, the Alabama National Guard was used. There were united struggles of Black and white miners throughout all the coal mines in Alabama, Black miners in most cases being in the majority on the picket lines or facing the county high sheriffs or the company armed gunmen or the National Guard. At some points the struggles turned into battlegrounds between the miners and the armed company thugs.

All kinds of dirty work were tried against the miners;

some of the company officials had their homes fired on in order to frame militant strikers who wouldn't be scared off by threats. Some newspapers harped on the "social equality" theme as one sure trick to break the strike unity of Black and white.

Many such struggles shaped up on Red Mountain among the red-ore miners, under the leadership of the Mine, Mill and Smelter Workers Union. The Raymond ore mine (Republic Steel) had the first Mine-Mill local organized up on Red Mountain. The first president of the local was Lewis Tarrant, Black, who was elected by white and Black members of the union in the Raymond mine. It was said that each year he wanted to resign but nobody else would agree to take on the job.

In mentioning various rank-and-filers who came forward to leadership in Birmingham, I have mentioned the names of several people who participated in the early struggles. There is one person I should give a lot more credit to for the role he played, and that is Sam Hall.

Sam Hall was born and raised in Alabama, around Anniston. After he came out of college and before he went into the army during World War II, he was a newspaper reporter. He had been active in the Party both in Birmingham and in Alabama generally before the war, editing a paper in Birmingham known as the *News Almanac.*

I had the good fortune of many meetings and discussions with him on union and political questions and on mass work, but especially on the right-to-vote movement in the South. Not only did I become very fond of him but I respected his leadership ability—particularly since he was a Southern-raised white worker. We could speak the same language together; we had a common understanding of the conditions in the South. He did a good bit of writing on the economic problems of the South, especially as they related to the Black people. Sam, along with

Mayfield and a few others, was with me when 1 had to leave Birmingham after "Bull" Connor began his raids against all radicals, and President Truman had started his Korean War in June 1950.

Sam and his wife Sylvia were making payments on a home they had bought in their native state, but they had to sell it. Mayfield was also buying a home and he also lost his. Both men had been buying under GI loans.

Sam and I came to New York, where we stayed for quite some time. Then he went to other parts of the South, just as I did. After a while he began having trouble with his head. The last time I saw him it was just before he was to go into the hospital to be operated on for brain tumor. We were down on the Hudson River bank at 110th Street, sitting in the bright sun talking, and I had a mimeographed copy of a first draft of this book. I wanted his opinion of it, but he said his head was bothering him and he didn't want to do any thinking. But he promised that as soon as he came out of the hospital, he would give it his consideration. Well, he never did read after the operation because he never recovered from it.

Sam was a wonderful Southern-born white worker. He was always a true partner when we worked together around Birmingham, both in the Party and in the mass movements.

As I now remember, the first white member of the Party I had met was Harry Sims, who was killed in the Kentucky minefields during a strike along about 1932. The second was Will Weinstone, a veteran Communist leader.

I met Will on a Christmas night, 1931. I had had a big time at a Christmas party—was feeling pretty happy. My wife told me somebody had left a message for me to come out to a friend's house in Woodlawn; somebody there wanted to see me. The man I met that night was

Weinstone. I thought he had the blackest hair I had ever seen; he talked in a strong, forthright way and was very serious-looking. I said to myself, this man sure means business.

Well, four or five of us were sitting around a table talking but I had had some drinks and was feeling sleepy. I tried my best to stay awake—everybody knew why I couldn't—and I felt embarrassed. To this day every time I see Will I think about that Christmas night in 1931 and how that good talk about the Scottsboro Case and the other issues of vital interest to me passed over my sleeping head. Fortunately my comrades did not hold it against me, but maybe I can add that my regret over the incident was part of my education.

14

THEN AND NOW

In these pages I have related some of the experiences of a Black worker in the South over a period covering roughly the first 70 years of the 20th century. It is a story of struggle against the harsh conditions, the cruel oppression of the Negro people—whether it was the life of a sharecropper's family wresting a bare subsistence from the soil, or that of an industrial worker up against the walls of discrimination and exploitation. It is also a story of struggle and the education that I got in the process —with the guidance of the Communist Party. I hope I have made it clear that I would never have been able to play my small part in the historic campaigns to defeat lynch justice, to build the union, and to win elementary civil rights without the fellow-workers and the progressive organizations that schooled us in struggle.

The Negro people will always be struggling and will always face setbacks until the time comes when all of us along with our white friends can join the ranks and organize the masses in their own defense. We'll continue to get a lot of lip-service from the higher-ups and from certain liberals, but struggle and unity remain our only real weapons.

If the working people knew their strength, they would not let themselves be pushed around and they wouldn't let themselves be divided. The agents of the capitalist class say we Communists are subversive, that we believe in the overthrow of the government by force and violence. As long as people are brainwashed into believing these lies, the enemy will be able to keep them suffering in slums, starving in the midst of plenty, being framed-up, jailed, bombed, lynched, buried in unknown graves. When the masses of people recognize the truth that liberation can be won—as millions are attaining it in socialist lands and moving toward it in hitherto oppressed nations—they will also recognize that the working class has no political representative other than the Communist Party. The two major parties cannot escape serving the big money interests. When the status quo is threatened, certain concessions may be granted by the ruling class, but basic change can come about only when the people own the means of production.

The year 1931 seems a very long time ago, but it was then, in Birmingham, Alabama, that nine boys were accused of raping two white girls on a freight train. They were tried in a lily-white court (Black people were denied the right to serve on juries just as they were denied all other civil rights). Violation of the Constitution, along with utter contempt for human rights, was the order of the day.

As I have recorded earlier, it was the International Labor Defense, supported by the Communist Party, that came to the defense of the Scottsboro boys after they had been sentenced to electrocution. The ILD never let up on the point that Black people had not served on the jury that handed down the death verdict, and that the constitutional right to a jury of one's peers was being violated. The case was appealed, and new trials were won over a long period of cruel ordeals for the nine youths.

In every leaflet and pamphlet issued by the ILD and the Party and distributed in Alabama and the rest of the South, demands were raised at all times for the right of Black people to vote and to be elected to office. And they called upon the people to organize and unite to win these and other rights.

Negroes and white people of the 12th Congressional District in Brooklyn, New York, in 1968 elected the first Black woman to Congress. I never dreamed that one day I would become a qualified voter and would have the privilege of helping to elect Mrs. Shirley Chisholm. I was particularly happy that this was achieved in my lifetime because, to me, it represented the culmination of decades of struggle in which I and so many others had participated.

In the flush of this impressive political victory, I could not help remembering a cold winter day in 1933 when fifteen of us, unemployed at the time, walked down to the Jefferson County Court House in Birmingham and told the officials we had come down to vote. An old man with a peg leg, whom we called Uncle Bud, was the spokesman for the group.

The officials of the court house, including the county sheriff and some of his deputies, gathered around us wanting to know who had sent us. Were we Reds? What did we want to vote for? Uncle Bud told them we wanted to vote someone into office who would give the unemployed some food and clothes. Finally we were told to go away, and they would see to the hungry people getting more food and clothing.

The *Birmingham Post* came out with big headlines saying that 50 hungry Negroes had marched on the County Court House and demanded the right to vote.

The struggle continued for years, and in 1938 we organized a right-to-vote club with the program of studying the Alabama State and U.S. Constitutions. We got a young white lawyer to go to the court house and get a copy of the registration blank and we mimeographed several hundred copies. We conducted classes, and our meetings were announced in the *Birmingham World*, the Black people's weekly paper. People from all walks of life attended—coal miners, steel workers, school teachers and many others. Every one of us, no matter how poorly we could read and write, learned the answers to the questions on the registration blank.

When we met with the same delaying tactics at the board of registrars, we made an arrangement with A. D. Shores, a Black attorney, that any person who had been denied his right to register or to vote should petition the courts for a hearing. In the end, there were so many Black people becoming voters as a result of filing these complaints, that the state legislature in Montgomery enacted the Boswell Amendment, which allowed the Registration Board to put any questions on the blanks they chose; they were then free to make it even harder for the Black people. Despite all these tricks, many Black men and women were able to complete the forms and to register.

In the meanwhile, the white politicians of Birmingham had called some of the Black leaders together and allowed them to organize the Negro Democratic Voters' Club. They gave them a charter after making an agreement with the Black leaders that they would help the white politicians to keep the poor Black and white

masses from getting together and going to the Communists for leadership. The Negroes were told that the
politicians would pass any of the Black friends they
brought down to the Board of Registrars. But they were
told not to bring any of the "common" Black people or
over fifty a year.

To counteract these devious schemes, nearly 200 Black
leaders from all parts of the South met in New Orleans,
Louisiana. We organized a Black people's nonpartisan
Democratic Voters' League for the entire South, under
the direction of Rev. A. M. Jackson. Thousands of Black
people became voters under the leadership of the Voters'
League.

And the following year, 1945, a united front conference of all the Black people's organizations in Birmingham was held in the U.S.O. Center to launch a campaign
to awaken the people to the importance of the franchise.
They agreed to raise a large amount of money to place a
full-page ad in all the Birmingham daily newspapers.
Various committees were set up to call on leading businesses, individuals and groups in the cities. The Rev. A.
Babbleton Johnson was appointed chairman of the committee to call on the labor unions of the city. I served on
that committee with him and we went to top union
leaders to ask for their help.

I have described a number of the other struggles we
waged for the right to organize and to vote. It is not
surprising that I had by now become a target for the
KKK and the bosses. In 1948 the KKK and some of the
steel union officials of Birmingham got me out of Local
2815, of which I had been president for six years. They
were able to silence my voice in the CIO union until
1950. In that year we organized in Bessemer and Birmingham in a united political action committee.

And late in 1950, "Bull" Connor, the "Birmingham
Bull," gave orders to his detectives to bring me in, but

before they made their move to get me, I got the word to lay low and I got out of sight of all his stooges on the streets. I remained in Birmingham until late 1951 and I met the friends I wanted to see when I was ready to meet them. Sometimes I would be on the city trolley with some of "Bull" Connor's agents, but they did not recognize me. I finally left and settled in Newark, New Jersey; later I went to work on a night job in New York. My night work kept me from being active, until I became a member of the Committee to Elect a Black Congresswoman from Brooklyn. When the members voted to draft a candidate for Congress from the 12th Congressional District, I was elected on the committee to interview the people who were chosen. When the committee chose Mrs. Chisholm, I fully supported her and I had great satisfaction in seeing her elected by an overwhelming majority. Perhaps you can see how great a victory this seemed to me after all the years of struggle.

When I visited in Atlanta and Birmingham in 1964, I couldn't believe some of the changes I saw. The Greyhound bus station had abolished its jimcrow toilets; Black men and white men were using the same washbowl. When I went for lunch, everyone was served at the same counter; we all went to the same window to buy tickets.

Beyond these and other social changes in the South, so long overdue and so hard fought for, throughout the country Black men were beginning to hold high office—as mayors, congressmen and in other political capacities. The level of education has risen, as thousands of young Negroes complete a college education; and the level of economic well-being for a small proportion of Blacks has also risen.

Nevertheless, I hold that into the Seventies the concessions that are being made through piecemeal measures will serve a limited purpose just so far and for just so long. In the meanwhile, the sufferings and oppression of the vast mass of Black, Chicano and Puerto Rican people remain at an increasingly unbearable level. Unemployment, lack of housing, ghetto misery, arrests, frame-ups, the murder of innocent men and women—all these increase, and only basic changes in the structure of society will solve these terrible conditions.

Within the last decade we have seen youth, Black and white, in motion, fighting for peace in Vietnam, rejecting the Government's imperialist adventures abroad and the oppression of working people at home. We have had Black youth and white struggling together side by side. Two white youths were buried in the same Mississippi fishdam as their Black brother. Other young whites have come forward (and some of their elders, too); they have suffered arrest; risked and lost their lives fighting on the side of Black liberation in the South.

You see, Negroes know who their friends are; it is not a question of suspicion and prejudice based on color—it is a question of conduct, and I am convinced that whites and Blacks who have common principles can, with determination, achieve unity in the life-and-death struggle for justice and freedom for all mankind.

For myself, I live in the present; I started struggling for human rights in the past; and, with the help of my Marxist education, I get bright glimpses of the future. I can see one thing above all else: in order to be successful in the struggle for full freedom, Black people in the South and throughout the United States must be organized, must be educated, learn how to be even more active in their own defense—indeed, in their fight for survival.

What gains we have won have grown out of the kind of organizations and campaigns I have described. My only real education came through the teachings of Marxism-

Leninism and the leadership of the Communist Party. What other party could possibly teach the people such understanding of politics as it taught me?

In conclusion, I want to add that I did not wage these struggles alone. I would not do justice to my readers or to myself if I failed to point out the role that was played by many Southern white workers in these struggles. Here I will name a few of the outstanding fighters for justice: the late Jane Speed, a young white woman from Montgomery; the late Sam Hall, a young white news reporter from Anniston, Alabama; the late Joseph Gelders, chairman of the Civil Liberties Committee of Birmingham; Mary Leonard, a white working-class woman of Birmingham—and many, many more who worked in these historic struggles.

It would be well for both Black and white youth today to study the important history of these united struggles as lessons that can be a guide to all youth in their efforts to resist oppression.

Black youth and adults as well have a special task to perform. One of the most deadly poisons that exists among us and keeps us divided is petty jealousy. In my long years of experience in the South and in the country as a whole, this has been one of the most effective weapons the Powers-that-be that own the wealth of this country have ever been able to plant among the Black people. They have used it to keep us divided and fighting among ourselves, preventing us from reaching the high point of full freedom, to which we have contributed so much of our blood and toil alongside the great mass of other working people. This disunity must be rooted out of our ranks if we are to be the great people we are striving to be. To every man and woman, boy and girl, in respect to leadership and high posts our slogan must be: to each according to his or her ability and not according to some individual's or some little group's claim to leadership.

The major slogan among the Black people in these perilous times must be to *unite*. I repeat this again and again because I know how our enemies try to divide us. We should unite Black people and above all the Black youth, not for a separate state in this country, not to hate the white youth and the poor white working masses, but to join with them because only through such unity will we be able to play our role as a force to make the wealth of our country benefit all the people, to enable them to live without hunger and want. To sum up the meaning of my seventy years of living, I would say that four words are sufficient: Learn, Struggle, Organize, Unite.

CPSIA information can be obtained
at www.ICGtesting.com
Printed in the USA
FSHW011605061020
74466FS